Teaching Social Issues with Film

Teaching Social Issues with Film

William Benedict Russell III
University of Central Florida

INFORMATION AGE PUBLISHING, INC.
Charlotte, NC • www.infoagepub.com

Library of Congress Cataloging-in-Publication Data

Russell, William B.
  Teaching social issues with film / William Benedict Russell.
    p. cm.
  Includes bibliographical references and index.
  ISBN 978-1-60752-116-7 (pbk.) – ISBN 978-1-60752-117-4 (hardcover)
  1. Social sciences–Study and teaching (Secondary)–Audio-visual aids. 2.
Social sciences–Study and teaching (Secondary)–Research. 3. Motion
pictures in education. I. Title.
  H62.2.R86 2009
  361.0071'2–dc22

                                                          2009024393

Printed in the United States of America

Contents

Preface and Overview

I don't seek out social issue films, but I am proud to be in a movie
that will make people think.

—Kevin Spacey, Academy Award–winning actor

Social issues have been depicted on the silver screen since the beginning of the film industry. George Eastman, the founder of Kodak, created flexible celluloid in 1888/89, which was the basis for motion picture film. Then, in 1891, Thomas Edison introduced the kinetoscope, a small peephole viewer for watching short and simple motion pictures. Eastman's creation of celluloid and Edison's kinetoscope helped spawn an era of silent films. Silent films were the only available films in the early 1900s, and it was not until 1929/30 that films with sound became readily available. During the silent film period many films dealt with a variety of social issues. Filmmakers such as George Tucker, Frank Powell, and most notably D.W. Griffith created films pertaining to various social issues like women's rights, divorce, racism, and poverty.

Filmmakers and performers alike have continued to create films that highlight various social issues. Many critics, viewers, and industry people would say that all films have a message, but they are not always noticeable or good. There are films that feature social issues as a primary or central focus, and it is those films that will be detailed in this volume because of their ability to help provoke thought and discussion among viewers.

Teaching Social Issues with Film, pages xiii–xv
Copyright © 2009 by Information Age Publishing
xiii

The primary focus of this volume is to encourage readers to teach with film. Chapter One, "Teaching with Film," provides readers with a research-based rationale for using film as an instructional tool in the classroom. Additionally, a general model for using film in the classroom, the *Russell Model for Using Film*, is detailed. This four-stage model will help ensure that teachers are utilizing film as an effective instructional tool.

Chapter Two, "Legal Issues," discusses the various legal issues and laws surrounding the use of film in the classroom. Specifically, Chapter Two discusses school district policies and copyright.

Chapter Three, "Teaching Social Issues with Film," discusses the need to teach social issues in the classroom and provides readers with a rationale for teaching social issues. Chapter Three discusses how teachers can use film to enhance the curriculum and increase student interest on various social issues. Furthermore, two different models for teaching social issues with film, the *Traditional Model* and the *Spring Board Model*, are detailed.

Chapter Four, "Evaluating Social Issues Films," discusses how to analyze and evaluate films. This chapter highlights media literacy-related skills and provides readers with generic media literacy questions. In addition, it discusses how teachers can evaluate social issues films and how students can evaluate social issues films.

Social issues are often controversial and divide the public. Social issues films can and will do the same. The majority of this volume is comprised of a filmography of social issues films. Chapter Five, "Filmography of Social Issues Films," is comprised of 180 films, each pertaining to one of the 30 social issues listed in the Table of Contents. The filmography is arranged alphabetically by social issue. Each social issue is explained, followed by a detailed listing of films relevant to the specific social issue. The films are arranged alphabetically by title. Each film entry includes bibliographic information and a film synopsis. Each social issue details six films. However, other films pertaining to each social issue are listed, but are not detailed.

Each film is grouped by its primary social issue. This volume is intended for teachers at the secondary and college level who are interested in teaching social issues with film. All 180 films were selected based on their relevance to the social issue and availability. Most of the films are available from public libraries or can be rented for a nominal charge from a video store. As well, all social issues films included in this volume are available for purchase on the Internet. Prices for films range from $.25 to $25.00 depending on format (VHS vs. DVD) and condition (used vs. new). Many are well under $10.00, if bought used, through online shopping websites such as Amazon (www.amazon.com).

Ideally, this volume will serve as a resource for those interested in promoting discussion, analysis, and critical thinking in the classroom through the examination of social issues using film.

William B. Russell III, PhD
University of Central Florida

Acknowledgments

I would like to express a sincere thank you to Catie, William, Juliet, Zeus, and all of my family and friends. I would also like to extend a thank you to the Motion Picture Association of America (MPAA) and University Press of America. I would also like to thank my PhD student and graduate research assistant, Stewart Waters.

Teaching Social Issues with Film, page xvii
Copyright © 2009 by Information Age Publishing
xvii

1

Teaching with Film

Teaching with film is considered a best practice and many consider teaching with film to be an effective strategy for teaching social studies content (Holmes, Russell, & Movitz, 2007; Russell, 2007a; Paris, 1997). Film can help students develop a better understanding of the content by providing visual images. In addition, Matz and Pingatore (2005) explain that film can bring students closer to a topic they are studying. Film is considered to be an effective communicator, and has the potential to arouse emotions (McPherson, in Russell, 2008), and stimulate feelings. With the current population of digital-savvy students, film is an essential part of life and popular culture. An average student spends over 7 hours a day using media. That is over 50 hours a week (Kaiser Family Foundation, 2005). Nearly 50% of student media use per day is exclusively devoted to videos (film) and television, a clear indication of how significant a role film, television, and other media play in a student's day-to-day life.

Film is an enhancement tool for the curriculum, but it is not the curriculum. Film has real-life applications and is relevant to students' everyday lives. Incorporating such a relevant tool into the curriculum can increase

Teaching Social Issues with Film, pages 1–5
Copyright © 2009 by Information Age Publishing
All rights of reproduction in any form reserved.

student interest in the material being studied, thus allowing it to become more meaningful and relevant to the student. Furthermore, authentic classroom activities help teachers achieve instructional goals such as retention, understanding, reasoning, and critical thinking (Driscoll, 2005). Not only are critical thinking skills encouraged by authentic film use, but also decision-making skills, especially when dealing with controversial social issues on film. Engle (2003) stressed decision making as the heart of social studies education, stressing that students learn the decision-making process, instead of content memorization. Decision-making skills can be honed by effectively teaching with film. Films help evoke meaningful inquiry of topics, which allows students to make insightful decisions based on what has been viewed and what the teacher does to support the curriculum. For film to be effective it must be used appropriately and not misused or abused.

Film is extremely popular and extremely accessible to students and teachers. In a research study of social studies teachers, 100% reported using film at least once a month to help teach social studies content (Russell, 2007b). In a 2006 study by Stoddard and Marcus, 92.9% of social studies teachers reported using film at least once a week. In 2006, a national survey of social studies teachers reported that 63% of eighth-grade teachers reported using some type of video-based activity in the last social studies class they taught (Leming, Ellington, & Schug, 2006). Additionally, in a national study of teachers, 69% of the teachers reported that they use some type of film/ movie to help teach Holocaust content. The method of using film to teach Holocaust content and the method of using firsthand accounts of the Holocaust were tied for the number one method teachers use (Donnelly, 2006).

The Russell Model for Using Film

The *Russell Model for Using Film* is a four-stage model for utilizing film in the classroom. Many teachers use film and think they use it effectively, but they do not follow the research-based guidelines for using film as laid out in the *Russell Model for Using Film* (see Table 1).

The Russell Model for Using Film

1. The Preparation Stage
2. The Previewing Stage
3. Watching the Film Stage
4. The Culminating Activity Stage

Many of the activities that are found in the *Russell Model for Using Film* have been found to help increase student achievement. Allen (1955) found

TABLE 1   The Russell Model for Using Film

Stage One: The Preparation Stage

The preparation stage is the planning stage of the *Russell Model for Using Film*. This stage is also considered the most important stage of the model. The preparation stage includes the following:

Required Activities
- Develop and create a lesson plan that incorporates film, while still meeting instructional goals/objectives and state standards.
- Adhere to all legal requirements.
- Preview the film! Instructors must preview all films before using a film in the classroom.
- Create specific activities needed for each stage (e.g., pre-viewing activity, culminating activity).
- Obtain permission from administration to use the film in the classroom.
- Obtain permission from students' parents/guardians to show the film in the classroom.
- Arrange for appropriate equipment needed (e.g., DVD/VCR player, LCD projector, TV).
- Arrange the classroom for viewing the film.

Stage Two: The Pre-Viewing Stage

The pre-viewing stage is done prior to students viewing the film in class. The pre-viewing stage includes the following:

Required Activities
- Introduce the film to students.
- Discuss the background of the film.
- Explain the purpose for viewing the film.
- Clearly connect the film to the topic/unit currently being studied.
- Introduce new vocabulary.
- Relate the film to students' prior knowledge.
- Relate the film to students' everyday lives.
- Relate the film to other content areas.
- Clarify any significant cinematic terminology (e.g., close-up, voice-over) that may impact the viewers' experience.
- Discuss what is required during the viewing of the film.
- Discuss the culminating activity that will follow the viewing of the film.
- Collect permission slips from parents/guardians. (Ideally, this should be done days/weeks prior to showing the film. Furthermore, administrative permission should be obtained prior to obtaining parent/guardian permission.)

Optional Activities
- Utilize a K-W-L chart: What I Know, What I Want to Know, and What I Learned.
- Read reviews/critiques of the film.
- Read interviews with the star/s, director, producer, etc.
- Have students read a synopsis of the film.

(continued)

TABLE 1   The Russell Model for Using Film (continued)

Stage Three: Watching the Film Stage
Watching the film stage is where students actually view the film. Showing the entire film is appropriate when necessary, as is showing small segments or clips. Research has been shown to support both types of film use. Stopping the film occasionally to highlight an important point, concept, issue, and/or scene is appropriate. The watching the film stage includes the following:

Required Activity
• Watch the film.

Optional Activities
• Have students take notes. (If notes are required, the teacher must provide ample light and time for writing the notes.)
• Complete a guided activity. (Some films have premade guided activities.)
• Answer questions created by the teacher.

Stage Four: The Culminating Activity Stage
The culminating activity stage is done after students have watched the film. The culminating activity stage includes the following:

Required Activities
• Stop the film.
• Review, clarify, and/or discuss major points, concepts, issues, scenes, and/or inaccuracies.
• Assess student learning (see assessment strategies).

Optional Assessment Strategies
• Class discussion
• Class debate
• Rewrite the ending of the film
• Write a review of the film
• Take a test/quiz
• Complete a written assignment aligned with the film and topic/unit
• Reenactment (have students reenact a scene from the film)
• Have students conduct a mock interview with the star, director, and/or producer of the film
• Have students analyze and evaluate the film

---

that if teachers announce a test during the previewing stage that students will learn more than those who were unaware of the test prior to showing the film. Allen also found that if teachers introduce and prepare the class for a film during the previewing stage, students retained more content information than students who did not receive the same introduction and preparation. Thus, it is crucial to make students aware of the requirements and clearly explain and clarify expectations. Informing students of expectations will help ensure the students' success.

By using the *Russell Model for Using Film*, teachers will help ensure that film is used to *enhance* the curriculum, not *as* the curriculum. Furthermore, teachers will help ensure that film is used appropriately and legally. The *Russell Model for Using Film* should be used as a guide; however, teachers still need to make sure that all professional, ethical, and legal standards are upheld.

Note

Sections and/or parts of this chapter were reprinted from Russell, W. (2007). *Using film in the social studies*. Lanham, MD: University Press of America Inc. Reprinted with permission.

2

Legal Issues

Many teachers use film in the classroom; however, they are unaware of the legal issues surrounding its appropriate use. It is extremely crucial that teachers understand and follow the law when using copyrighted materials. The two main legal issues surrounding the use of film in the classroom are (1) school/school district policies and regulations and (2) copyright.

School/district policies and regulations should be upheld. Since policies and regulations change from school to school and district to district, teachers need to check with school/district administrators to obtain the policies and regulations for using film in the classroom.

As stated above, policies and regulations for using film in the classroom change from school to school and district to district. A basic policy for using film in the classroom will be similar to the following:

1. All films must be used in the classroom for instructional purposes.
2. Films with a rating of "G" may be used for instructional purposes with teacher approval and administrative permission.

Teaching Social Issues with Film, pages 7–10
Copyright © 2009 by Information Age Publishing
All rights of reproduction in any form reserved.

3. Films with a rating of "PG" may be used for instructional purposes with teacher approval, administrative permission, and parent/ guardian permission.
4. Films with a rating of "PG-13" may be used for instructional purposes with teacher approval, administrative permission, and parent/guardian permission.
5. Films with a rating of "R" and/or higher cannot be shown. (See Appendix A for a detailed explanation of the MPAA film ratings.)

This basic policy is not applicable to all schools and/or school districts. Many times school districts will allow films with a rating of "R" to be used with approval from the school board. R-rated films that are commonly approved by school boards are *Schindler's List* and *Glory*.

Federal copyright laws are established by the United States Copyright Office. Section 110 (1) of Title 17 of the United States Code on Copyright and Conditions cites the following exemption for the use of copyrighted films for educational purposes:

> Performance or display of a work by instructors or pupils in the course of face-to-face teaching activities of a nonprofit educational institution, in a classroom or similar place devoted to instruction, unless in the case of a motion picture or other audiovisual work, the performance, or the display of individual images, is given by means of a copy that was not lawfully made under this title, and that the person responsible for the performance knew or had reason to believe was not lawfully made. (www.copyright.gov/title17/92chap1.html#110)

Simply put, a film must be used in a nonprofit educational institution, in an instructional class that is meeting face-to-face, and for educational purposes, not for entertainment or recreation. As well, educators can use a film that has been rented at a video store, borrowed from a library, and/or purchased, as long as the above regulations are adhered to.

Teachers should not make copies of films, use films as public performance, and/or make a profit from showing films. However, teachers can make copies of public television programs for educational use in the classroom. This practice is covered under the fair use code of copyrighted material. What is fair use? Section 107 of Title 17 (1) of the United States Code on Copyright and Conditions explains the fair use guidelines for the use of copyrighted materials for educational purposes:

> Notwithstanding the provisions of sections 106 and 106A, the fair use of a copyrighted work, including such use by reproduction in copies or phonorecords or by any other means specified by that section, for purposes such as

criticism, comment, news reporting, teaching (including multiple copies for classroom use), scholarship, or research, is not an infringement of copyright. In determining whether the use made of a work in any particular case is a fair use the factors to be considered shall include—

- the purpose and character of the use, including whether such use is of a commercial nature or is for nonprofit educational purposes;
- the nature of the copyrighted work;
- the amount and substantiality of the portion used in relation to the copyrighted work as a whole; and
- the effect of the use upon the potential market for or value of the copyrighted work

(www.copyright.gov/title17/92chap1.html#107)

The complete United States Code on Copyright and Conditions can be accessed via the Internet at www.copyright.gov/title17/.

Furthermore, to qualify as fair use, the Federal Guidelines for Off-Air Recording of Broadcast Programming for Educational Purposes (U.S. Government, 1981) should be adhered to. Those guidelines are as follows:

1. The guidelines were developed to apply only to off-air recording by nonprofit educational institutions.
2. A broadcast program may be recorded off-air simultaneously with broadcast transmission—(including simultaneous cable re-transmission) and retained by a nonprofit educational institution for a period not to exceed the first forty-five (45) consecutive calendar days after date of recording. Upon conclusion of such retention period, all off-air recordings must be ceased or destroyed immediately. "Broadcast programs" are television programs transmitted by television stations for reception by the general public without charge.
3. Off-air recordings may be used by individual teachers in the course of relevant teaching activities, and repeated once only when instructional reinforcement is necessary, in classrooms and similar places devoted to instruction within a single building, cluster, or campus, as well as in the homes of students receiving formalized home instruction, during the first ten (10) consecutive school days in the forty-five (45) calendar day retention period. "School days" are school session days—not counting weekends, holidays, vacations, examination periods, or other scheduled interruptions—within the forty-five (45) calendar day retention period.
4. Off-air recordings may be made only at the request of and used by individual teachers, and may not be regularly recorded in anticipation of requests. No broadcast program may be recorded off-air

more than once at the request of the same teacher, regardless of the number of times the program may be broadcast.

5. A limited number of copies may be reproduced from each off-air recording to meet the legitimate needs of teachers under these guidelines. Each such additional copy shall be subject to all provisions governing the original recording.

6. After the first ten (10) consecutive school days, off-air recordings may be used up to the end of the forty-five (45) calendar day retention period only for teacher evaluation purposes, i.e., to determine whether or not to include the broadcast program in the teaching curriculum, and may not be used in the recording institution for student exhibition or any other non-evaluation purpose without authorization.

7. Off-air recordings need not be used in their entirety, but the recorded programs may not be altered from their original content. Off-air recordings may not be physically or electronically combined or merged to constitute teaching anthologies or compilations.

8. All copies of off-air recordings must include the copyright notice on the broadcast programs as recorded.

9. Educational Institutions are expected to establish the appropriate control procedures to maintain the integrity of these guidelines. (p. E4750–E4752)

Note

Sections and/or parts of this chapter were reprinted from Russell, W. (2007). *Using film in the social studies*. Lanham, MD: University Press of America Inc. Reprinted with permission.

3

Teaching Social Issues with Film

Questions unite, answers divide
—Elie Wiesel

The practice of teaching social issues is often regarded as a best practice. However, teaching social issues is often a practice that teachers tend not to utilize. Typically, teachers shy away from social issues because they are often controversial in nature. Although controversial, the teaching of social issues is a powerful and effective method of instruction. As well, teaching controversial issues is a highly regarded and encouraged practice when done appropriately. The National Council for the Social Studies (NCSS; 2007) states the following:

> Controversial issues must be studied in the classroom without the assumption that they are settled in advance or there is only one right answer in matters of dispute. The social studies teacher must approach such issues in a spirit of critical inquiry exposing the students to a variety of ideas, even if they are different from their own.

Furthermore, the National Council for the Social Studies outlines the following specific skills and attitudes that are developed through the study of controversial social issues:

1. The ability to study relevant social problems of the past or present and make informed decisions or conclusions;
2. The ability to use critical reasoning and evidence-based evaluation in the study and analysis of significant issues and ideas; this includes development of skills of critical analysis and evaluation in considering ideas, opinions, information, and sources of information;
3. The recognition that differing viewpoints are valuable and normal as a part of social discourse;
4. The recognition that reasonable compromise is often an important part of the democratic decision-making process.

No matter the position of the National Council for the Social Studies, many classroom teachers eliminate controversial social issues from the curriculum. Byford, Lennon, and Russell (2008) explained that teachers tend not to teach controversial subjects because (1) teachers lack the appropriate classroom management skills, (2) restrictive school/district policies, (3) the teachers' comfort level of discussing various issues, and (4) job security. Levitt and Longstreet (1993) explain that many teachers consider teaching controversial issues a "no-win" situation, because once the controversial issues reflect reality, the results could be counterproductive to students. In addition, Cotton (2006) concluded that teachers found difficulty in avoiding stating opinions themselves or becoming actively involved in the argument and debate.

The teaching of controversial social issues is not only met with trepidation by teachers, but also by pre-service teachers. Misco and Patterson (2007) reported that many pre-service teachers are uncomfortable teaching controversial issues related to sexual orientation, sexual harassment, and/or religion. The teaching of controversial social issues is almost nonexistent in many classrooms. Kahne, Rodriguez, Smith, and Thiede (2000) observed 8th- and 10th-grade social studies classes and found an almost complete absence of opportunities for students to discuss and analyze controversial social issues. Byford and colleagues (2008) examined high school social studies teachers ($N = 67$) and concluded that 75% reported that controversial issues should be taught; however, over 65% reported feeling unable to effectively teach controversial issues. This is because many teachers do not know how to effectively teach controversial social issues and they do not have the appropriate resources available to effectively teach controversial material, such as social issues films.

Controversial social issues can be an effective teaching tool in the classroom. Examining controversial social issues can help students learn to deal with conflict and take on life's leadership roles (Soley, 1996), and may teach students to clarify and justify their opinions on a number of issues. In today's society, students are often unable to justify their own opinions and debate various issues with rational reasoning. When dealing with political and social issues students typically accept their parents and/or close relatives' opinions and views as their own, without giving any real thought to the issues at hand (Russell, 2004). Teaching controversial social issues allows students to be actively engaged in the curriculum and allows the issues to become more meaningful and relevant to students' everyday lives (McGowan, McGowan, & Lumbard, 1994; Torney-Purta, Lehman, Oswald, & Schulz, 2002). Additionally, discussing controversial social issues can help students develop critical decision-making skills, and decision making is considered the heart of social studies education (Engle, 2003).

Social issues films should not be used as the final authority on an issue, but more as a tool to promote discussion and thinking about an issue. For example, when *Bowling for Columbine* was released, many people started asking questions about school violence, gun control, and the Second Amendment. Whether the movie accurately informed viewers is up for debate. However, what is not debatable is the fact that the film inspired viewers to think and discuss the issues at hand. Classroom teachers should not be concerned with promoting their personal political and/or social agenda, because this often gets teachers in trouble and can be detrimental to students. Instead, teachers should encourage basic decision-making skills and focus on the process of examining social issues, not necessarily the outcome.

To help ensure appropriate film use, refer to the *Russell Model for Using Film* in Chapter Two. The *Russell Model* should be used in conjunction with the following two models when teaching social issues with film. Due to the controversial nature and the need for specialized instruction, teaching social issues needs to be treated slightly differently than other curriculum. The following two models will ensure that teachers effectively teach social issues with film.

The Traditional Model (see Table 2) allows teachers to establish the curriculum and utilize a social issue film as a means to teach social issues. The *Traditional Model* uses a social issue film as a visually stimulating tool and a visual information source. Oftentimes the curriculum plan will include specific assignments and/or discussions relating directly to the film. However,

---

TABLE 2   The Traditional Model for Teaching Social Issues with Film

Phase One: Orientation
- The social issue is presented to students.
- Various stances on the issue are presented.
- The film is introduced using the procedures outlined in Stage 2 of the *Russell Model for Using Film.*

Phase Two: View Social Issue Film
- Students view the social issue film (whole film or clips of film can be used).
- Students complete film viewing activity (optional).

Phase Three: Self-Reflection
- Students reflect upon their own views.
- Students reflect upon the origination of their own views.
- Students reflect upon the influences on their views.

Phase Four: Exploration
- Students explore all sides of the issue using various resources (e.g. books, films, Internet, etc.).
- Students explore all sides of the issue using various methods (debate, role-playing, discussion, etc.).

Phase Five: Justification
- Students reach a decision.
- Students justify that decision with evidence.

Phase Six: Culmination
- Students and teacher reflect on the process.
- Students share their decision with the whole class (optional).

---

this is not a requirement. Typically, the entire film or a moderately sized section of the film is viewed. However, this depends on the teacher, the lesson objectives, and the students' individual needs.

The *Spring Board Model* (see Table 3) utilizes social issues films differently than the *Traditional Model.* In this model, social issues films or film clips are used as a way to introduce a social issue. The film's depiction of the social issue will heighten student interest with the issue and promote active participation. Typically, when using the *Spring Board Model* teachers only utilize brief film clips, instead of the entire film. However, there are instances when the entire film would be appropriate. This depends on the teacher, the lesson objectives, and the students' individual needs.

Although not specified, Stage One: The Preparation Stage of the *Russell Model for Using Film* should be adhered to when implementing the *Traditional Model* and/or the *Spring Board Model.*

TABLE 3   The Spring Board Model for Teaching Social Issues with Film

Phase One: View Social Issue Film
- Students view the social issue film (whole film or clips of film can be used).
- Students complete film viewing activity (optional).

Phase Two: Self-Reflection
- Students reflect upon their own views.
- Students reflect upon the origination of their own views.
- Students reflect upon the influences on their views.

Phase Three: Exploration
- Students explore all sides of the issue using various resources (e.g., books, films, Internet, etc.).
- Students explore all sides of the issue using various methods (debate, role playing, discussion, etc.).

Phase Four: Justification
- Students reach a decision.
- Students justify that decision with evidence.

Phase Five: Culmination
- Students and teacher reflect on the process.
- Students share their decision with the whole class (optional).

4

Evaluating Social Issues Films

Evaluating Social Issues Films

Using film as an instructional teaching method is a common practice. However, film education is not common. Teachers are not prepared to effectively use film as an instructional tool and students are not prepared to effectively view films and make informed decisions with regards to the content of the film. In a recent study, 100% of social studies teachers reported using film at least once a month. As well, 51% reported using film at least two to three times a month, some even reported using film four to five times a month or six or more times a month (Russell, 2007b). Despite the abundance of film use, the majority of teachers have never been properly trained to use film effectively and appropriately.

A simple and effective way to prepare teachers and students to utilize film is for them to become media literate. Media literacy is a major component of teaching social issues with film. Becoming media literate helps individuals become more informed citizens. Many films, along with other types of media (print and nonprint) can influence an individual's attitudes, beliefs, and/or values. The influence is so strong it is often not repudiated and the information is deemed accurate and creditable. Thus individuals adopt the

Teaching Social Issues with Film, pages 17–21

information as their own, without truly exploring the topic and making their own informed decision. Social issues films, like other types of media, should not be used as a final authority. Instead, the films should be used to promote critical thinking and discussion. Incorporating media literacy components into lessons that utilize film enables students to gain a more comprehensive understanding with regards to the film and the content.

Media Literacy

Media literacy is one of the most important skills for teachers and students to obtain. It is an essential aspect of any lesson that utilizes film or any other type of media. Media literacy is simply the ability to analyze and evaluate all types of media. However, a more specific and robust definition has been developed by the Center for Media Literacy (CML). The CML (2009a) states:

> Media Literacy is a 21st century approach to education. It provides a framework to access, analyze, evaluate and create messages in a variety of forms—from print to video to the Internet. Media literacy builds an understanding of the role of media in society as well as essential skills of inquiry and self-expression necessary for citizens of a democracy.

Furthermore, teaching students media literacy skills have numerous benefits including the following outlined by the Center for Media Literacy (2009b):

1. **Meets the needs of students to be wise consumers of media,** managers of information and responsible producers of their ideas using the powerful multimedia tools of a global media culture.
2. **Engages students**...bringing the world of media into the classroom connects learning with "real life" and validates their media culture as a rich environment for learning.
3. **Gives students and teachers alike a common approach to critical thinking** that, when internalized, becomes second nature for life.
4. **Provides an opportunity for integrating all subject areas** and creating a common vocabulary that applies across all disciplines.
5. **Helps meet state standards** while, at the same time using fresh contemporary media content which students love.
6. **Increases the ability and proficiency of students** to communicate (express) and disseminate their thoughts and ideas in a wide (and growing) range of print and electronic media forms—and even international venues.

7. **Media literacy's "inquiry process" transforms teaching** and frees the teacher to learn along with students—becoming a "guide on the side" rather than a "sage on the stage."

8. **By focusing on process skills rather than content knowledge**, students gain the ability to analyze *any* message in *any* media and thus are empowered for living all their lives in a media-saturated culture.

These skills will enable teachers and students to appropriately analyze and evaluate various forms of media, which will help move the learning process beyond the rote memorization of facts.

> To become media literate is not to memorize facts or statistics about the media, but rather to learn to raise the right questions about what you are watching, reading or listening to. (CML, 2009c)

This questioning ability that media literacy promotes will prove valuable in the classroom and in life. Helping students ask questions and think critically, which are key components to the decision-making process.

Teacher Evaluation of Social Issues Films

Evaluating social issues films needs to be done at two different levels. The first level of evaluation is for the teacher. Teachers need to be able to analyze and evaluate social issues films for educational appropriateness, potential, value, and relevance. Evaluating for educational appropriateness should be as simple as using common sense. As stated in Stage One of the *Russell Model for Using Film* (see Table 1), teachers need to ensure that they are adhering to the school/district guidelines for using film in the classroom. Teachers also need to be sure to obtain administrative and parental permission. Evaluating social issues films for educational potential, value, and relevance is more subjective to the individual instructor and the individual needs and abilities of the students. When evaluating social issues films, teachers should view the film and determine its educational value. The educational value needs to fit the curriculum and the needs of the students. The more relevant the film and instruction, the more meaningful and powerful the lesson will be.

To help teachers evaluate films for educational potential, it is recommended that the Film Analysis Sheet (see Appendix B) be utilized. This is a generic form that can be utilized with most films.

Student Evaluation of Social Issues Films

Once the teacher evaluates a film and decides to implement it into the curriculum, the evaluation process shifts to the students. However, before students can effectively analyze and evaluate films, they need to be trained.

Training students to evaluate film is the foundation for successfully learning from film. Students need to understand basic film terminology (see Appendix C) and media literacy skills. To help sharpen students' media literacy skills, use the following "Media Literacy Questions." These are generic media literacy questions that can be used for any film and can be tailored for other types of media.

■ Who made this film?
■ When was this film created?
■ What is the purpose of this film?
■ Who supported/sponsored this film?
■ What is the target audience of this film?
■ How is this film made for that audience?
■ What cinematic techniques were used?
■ Why were these techniques used?
■ What is this film implying or saying about the issue, event, person, place, etc., that is being portrayed?
■ What is missing from this film?

These questions are simple, but powerful. To demonstrate how these questions work, here are a few examples:

Example 1: *Schindler's List.* Who made this film? Steven Spielberg. When explored, this answer provides a great deal of information. It is a well-known fact that Steven Spielberg is Jewish. This could impact the film's depiction of specific issues, people, events, and/or time periods.

Example 2: *The Passion of the Christ.* Who made this film? Mel Gibson. When explored, this answer provides a great deal of information. It is well documented that Mel Gibson is a devoted Catholic and has publicly demonstrated prejudice toward Jewish people. This could impact the film's depiction of the specific issues, people, events, and/or time periods.

These questions help bring to the surface issues, concerns, and/or possible bias held within and around the film. It is this questioning ability that allows individuals to make their own informed decisions. By asking media literacy-type questions students will gain a more clear and comprehensive understanding of the film.

It should be noted that creating a feature-length film is considered an art. Films are written, directed, acted, and produced by people that have different attitudes, beliefs, and values. By training students to read the film, students will be better prepared to analyze and evaluate the film and decipher what is meaningful and what is not. Included in the analysis and evaluation of social issues films is the need for students to understand basic film terminology. By understanding film terminology, students will have a better grasp of various cinematic techniques that directors use to engage and influence viewers. Whether it is as common and recognizable as music, or as complex as fancy editing techniques, either way, understanding basic film terminology will strengthen students' ability to analyze and evaluate film. For a list of film terminology, see Appendix C.

5

Filmography of Social Issues Films

The filmography of social issues films is simply a list of films pertaining to various social issues. This filmography does not include every film ever made that deals with social issues, but rather it does include films that clearly depict or relate to a specific social issue. Furthermore, all 180 films were selected based on their relevance to the social issue, instructional use, and availability. The majority of the films can be found at a local video rental store or can be purchased from an online store (e.g., www.amazon.com) for a nominal price.

This filmography includes feature-length films and documentaries. Films categorized as home movies, government films, and educational films have been excluded from this filmography. Each film is grouped by its primary social issue; however, many of the films provided deal with multiple social issues. This volume is intended for teachers at the secondary and college level who are interested in teaching social issues with film. The social issues are arranged alphabetically and a brief definition/explanation of the social issue is provided. Each social issue details six films, arranged alphabetically by title. However, other films pertaining to the social issue

Teaching Social Issues with Film, pages 23–162
Copyright © 2009 by Information Age Publishing
All rights of reproduction in any form reserved.

are listed, but not detailed. Each film entry includes a film synopsis and the following bibliographic information: year, genre, Motion Picture Association of America (MPAA) rating, alternative title/s, director, producer, writer, length, language, color, company, and cast.

Some of the films detailed in this volume may not be appropriate to show in full in a secondary classroom. Ultimately, teachers must determine the appropriateness and educational value of the film for their instructional needs. Thus, teachers need to ensure that they are adhering to school/district procedures related to teaching with film. As with any type of classroom instruction, teachers need to ensure that the curriculum and instruction meets the learning goals/objectives of the lesson and the individual needs of the students.

Abortion

Abortion, simply put, is the removal of a fetus or embryo from a woman's uterus. The removal can be done medically, surgically, or by other means. Currently abortion is one of the most controversial social issues in society. The issue is divided into pro-life and pro-choice regimes. Although many are torn on the issue, abortion is an important topic during the election of government officials and among religious groups. Films relevant to this topic can pertain to other social issues, such as women's rights and teen pregnancy. However, these social issues are handled separately in this chapter.

Other films dealing with abortion not detailed in this volume include: *Blue Denim* (1955), *The Cardinal* (1963), *Cider House Rules* (1999), *Detective Story* (1951), *Finn's Girl* (2007), *The Interns* (1962), *Leona's Sister Gerri* (1995), *Live Free or Die* (2000), *Patty* (1962), *Prophecy* (1979), *Rosita* (2005), *To Find a Man* (1972), *Unborn in the USA: Inside the War on Abortion* (2007), and *10 Rillington Place* (1971).

A PRIVATE MATTER

(1992)

Genre: Drama

MPAA Rating: PG-13

Alternative Title: *Miss Sherri*

Directed By: Joan Micklin Silver

Produced By: Ronnie D. Clemmer, Lindsay Doran, Bill Pace, and Sydney Pollack

Written By: William Nicholson

Color: Color

Length: 118 minutes

Language: English

Production Company: Home Box Office

Cast: Sissy Spacek, Aidan Quinn, Estelle Parsons, Sheila McCarthy, Leon Russom, and Xander Berkeley

Film Synopsis

A Private Matter is based on the true story of *Romper Room* host Sherri Finkbine. Sherri (Sissy Spacek) has a sleeping disorder and is prescribed a drug, which is being blamed for causing birth defects. When Sherri finds that she is pregnant, she is faced with the decision of having a baby who could have birth defects, or having an abortion. Sherri decides having an abortion is the best option and her decision sets off a community and media frenzy.

THE CHOICE

(1981)

Genre: Drama

MPAA Rating: Not Rated

Alternative Title: None

Directed By: David Greene

Produced By: David Greene

Written By: Dennis Nemec

Color: Color

Length: 95 minutes

Language: English

Production Company: David Greene Productions

Cast: Susan Clark, Mitch Ryan, Largo Woodruff, Kathleen Lloyd, Lisa Jane Persky, and Paul Regina

Film Synopsis

Lisa Clements (Largo Woodruff) is **pregnant**. Lisa keeps her pregnancy a secret from her boyfriend Michael (Paul **Regina**). While visiting her parents, Lisa tells her mother, Kay (Susan **Clark**), about her pregnancy. Kay reveals that she secretly had an abortion and explains the reasons behind her choice. After hearing her mother's story, Lisa decides to tell Michael about the pregnancy.

IF THESE WALLS COULD TALK

(1996)

Genre: Drama

MPAA Rating: R

Alternative Title: None

Directed By: Cher and Nancy Savoca

Produced By: Demi Moore and Suzanne Todd

Written By: Pamela Wallace, Earl Wallace, Nancy Savoca, Susan Nanus, and I. Marlene King

Color: Color

Length: 96 minutes

Language: English

Production Company: HBO NYC Productions

Cast: Demi Moore, Sissy Spacek, Catherine Keener, Anne Heche, Jada Pinkett Smith, Cher, Jason London, and Kevin Cooney

Film Synopsis

If These Walls Could Talk is comprised of three different stories about women who occupy the same house over a span of 40 years. All three women deal with unplanned pregnancy and struggle over the question of having an abortion. The first story is set in 1952, and focuses on Claire Donnelly (Demi Moore), a widowed nurse, and her unplanned pregnancy. The second story is set in 1974 and is about Barbara Barrows' (Sissy Spacek) unplanned pregnancy and the options she has as a married housewife and mother of four. The third story is set in 1996 and focuses on Christine Cullen (Anne Heche), an unmarried college student, and her unplanned pregnancy.

LAKE OF FIRE

(2006)

Genre: Documentary

MPAA Rating: Not Rated

Alternative Title: None

Directed By: Tony Kaye

Produced By: Tony Kaye

Written By: Tony Kaye

Color: Black and white

Length: 152 minutes

Language: English

Production Company: Anonymous Content

Cast: Flip Benham, John Britton, Pat Buchanan, Noam Chomsky, Alan M. Dershowitz, and Michael F. Griffin

Film Synopsis

Lake of Fire is a graphic documentary film that examines and explores both the pro-life and pro-choice sides of abortion. Filmed in black and white, *Lake of Fire* is a collage of procedure footage, abortion-related discussions, personal stories, political statements, and individual interviews.

ROE VS. WADE

(1989)

Genre: Drama

MPAA Rating: Not Rated

Alternative Title: None

Directed By: Gregory Hoblit

Produced By: Gregory Hoblit

Written By: Alison Cross

Color: Color

Length: 100 minutes

Language: English

Production Company: NBC Productions

Cast: Holly Hunter, Amy Madigan, Kevin Cooney, Kathy Bates, James Gammon, and Alie Grant

Film Synopsis

Roe vs. Wade is based on the real-life events leading to the 1973 landmark Supreme Court decision, which legalized abortion in the first 6 months of pregnancy.

VERA DRAKE

(2004)

Genre: Drama/Crime

MPAA Rating: R

Alternative Title: None

Directed By: Mike Leigh

Produced By: Simon Channing-Williams and Alain Sarde

Written By: Mike Leigh

Color: Color

Length: 125 minutes

Language: English

Production Company: Les Films Alain Sarde

Cast: Imelda Staunton, Phil Davis, Richard Graham, Eddie Marsan, Daniel Mays, and Alex Kelly

Film Synopsis

Vera Drake is set in London, England, in the 1950s. Vera (Imelda Staunton) is a selfless woman willing to help any and all in need. Her services include inducing miscarriages in women with unwanted pregnancies. Although the practice is illegal, Vera feels she is doing the right thing. Vera's world starts to fall apart when complications occur during a procedure and the woman is forced to go to a hospital. The authorities are alerted and the police investigate Vera.

Addiction

Addiction is a common theme in many Hollywood films. Addiction is often portrayed in three main forms: alcohol addiction, drug addiction, and gambling addiction. Although there are many other forms of addiction portrayed in films, such as food addiction (*Can't Stop Eating* [2006] and *I Want Someone to Eat Cheese With* [2007]) and sex addiction (*I Am a Sex Addict* [2005], *A Dirty Shame* [2004], and *Certifiable* [2008]), the films pertained in this section deal with alcohol, drug, and gambling addiction.

Other films dealing with alcohol addiction not detailed in this volume include: *28 Days* (2000), *Arthur* (1983), *Blind Spot* (1947), *The Bottom of the Bottle* (1956), *Clean and Sober* (1988), *Dark Chocolate* (2008), *The Days of Wine and Roses* (1962), *Harvey* (1950), *Long Day's Journey into Night* (1962), *The Lost Weekend* (1945), *Papa's Delicate Condition* (1963), and *Smash-Up* (1947).

Other films dealing with drug addiction not detailed in this volume include the following: *Basketball Diaries* (1995), *Cristiane F.* (1981), *Drugstore Cowboy* (1989), *Facing the Habit* (2007), *FIX: The Story of an Addicted City* (2002), *A Hateful Rain* (1957), *Life or Meth* (2007), *The Man with the Golden Arm* (1956), *Monkey on My Back* (1957), *Opiated: Life Beneath the Eyelids* (2007), *Pure* (2002), *Ray* (2004), *Requiem for a Dream* (2000), *Sid & Nancy* (1986), *Spun* (2002), *Story of a Junkie* (1987), *Synanon* (1965), *Trainspotting* (1996), *Walk the Line* (2005), and *Way Out* (1967).

Other films dealing with gambling addiction not detailed in this volume include the following: *The Bet* (1992), *California Split* (1974), *Confessions of a Gambler* (2007), *The Great Sinner* (1949), *House of Games* (1987), *Hustle* (2004), *The Lady Gambles* (1949), and *$pent* (2000).

CANDY

(2006)

Genre: Drama/Romance

MPAA Rating: R

Alternative Title: None

Directed By: Neil Armfield

Produced By: Emile Sherman and Margaret Fink

Written By: Neil Armfield

Color: Color

Length: 108 minutes

Language: English

Production Company: Film Finance

Cast: Abbie Cornish, Heath Ledger, Geoffrey Rush, Tom Budge, Roberto Meza-Mont, Tony Martin, Noni Hazlehurst, Holly Austin, and Craig Moraghan

Film Synopsis

Candy is an Australian film about life, love, and drugs. A poet named Dan (Heath Ledger) falls in love with Candy (Abbie Cornish). The couple enjoys a Bohemian lifestyle and eventually become addicted to heroin. The film depicts their relationship, their drug use, and their decline. *Candy* was adapted for the screen from the book *Candy: A Novel of Love and Addiction* by Luke Davies.

LEAVING LAS VEGAS

(1995)

Genre: Drama/Romance

MPAA Rating: R

Alternative Title: None

Directed By: Mike Figgis

Produced By: Lila Cazès, Mark Fishcher, Stuart Regen, Paige Simpson, and Annie Stewart

Written By: Mike Figgis

Color: Color

Length: 118 minutes

Language: English, Russian

Production Company: Initial Productions

Cast: Nicholas Cage, Elisabeth Shue, Julian Sands, Richard Lewis, Steven Weber, Kim Adams, Emily Procter, Stuart Regen, and Valeria Golino

Film Synopsis

Leaving Las Vegas depicts the relationship between Ben Sanderson (Nicholas Cage), a suicidal alcoholic who traveled to Las Vegas to commit suicide via alcohol consumption, and Sera (Elisabeth Shue) a Las Vegas prostitute. *Leaving Las Vegas* is based on the semi-autobiographical book, *Leaving Las Vegas* by John O'Brien. It was nominated for four Academy Awards, in which it won one for Best Actor in a Leading Role (Nicholas Cage).

LUCKY GIRL

(2001)

Genre: Drama

MPAA Rating: Not Rated

Alternative Title: *My Daughter's Secret Life*

Directed By: John Fawcett

Produced By: Louise Garfield, Anne Marie La Traverse, and Claire Welland

Written By: Graeme Manson

Color: Color

Length: 100 minutes

Language: English

Production Company: Alliance Atlantis Communications

Cast: Elisha Cuthbert, Sherry Miller, Evan Sabba, Greg Ellwand, Sarah Osmond, Jonathan Whittaker, Charlotte Sullivan, Victoria Snow, and Jordan Walker

Film Synopsis

Lucky Girl is a Canadian television film about a 17-year-old girl named Kaitlin Palmerston (Elisha Cuthbert) who becomes addicted to gambling. Kaitlin is an upper-middle-class teenager with a gambling addiction that progresses throughout the film into a serious and potentially harmful vice. Eventually her addiction consumes her and she begins to borrow money from loan sharks and steal from friends and family.

MY NAME IS BILL W.

(1989)

Genre: Drama

MPAA Rating: Not Rated

Alternative Title: None

Directed By: Daniel Petrie

Produced By: Peter Duchow and James Garner

Written By: William G. Borchert

Color: Color

Length: 100 minutes

Language: English

Production Company: Garner-Duchow Productions

Cast: James Woods, JoBeth Williams, James Garner, Gary Sinise, George Coe, Robert Harper, Ray Reinhardt, Fritz Weaver, and Rick Warner

Film Synopsis

My Name is Bill W. is a CBS television movie based on a true story. The film depicts the life of Bill Wilson (James Woods) and how it was torn apart from the stock market crash and alcoholism. Eventually Wilson, along with fellow alcoholic, Dr. Robert Holbrook Smith (James Garner), creates a support group called Alcoholics Anonymous. *My Name is Bill W.* was nominated for seven Emmy Awards, in which it won one for Outstanding Lead Actor (James Woods).

OWNING MAHOWNY

(2003)

Genre: Drama

MPAA Rating: R

Alternative Title: None

Directed By: Richard Kwietniowski

Produced By: Alessandro Camon, Andras Hamori, and Seaton McLean

Written By: Maurice Chauvet

Color: Color

Length: 104 minutes

Language: English

Production Company: Alliance Atlantis Communications

Cast: Philip Seymour Hoffman, Minnie Driver, John Hurt, Maury Chaykin, Ian Tracey, Sonja Smits, K.C. Collins, and Vince Corazza

Film Synopsis

Owning Mahowny is based on the true story of the largest one-man bank fraud in Canadian history. The film depicts the story of Dan Mahowny (Philip Seymour Hoffman), a bank manager with access to millions of dollars, and his addiction to gambling. Over an 18-month period, Dan uses bank money to fund his gambling addiction, which eventually causes the destruction of his relationship, job, and life. The film's screenplay was based on the best-selling book *Stung* by Gary Ross.

THE PANIC IN NEEDLE PARK

(1971)

Genre: Drama

MPAA Rating: R

Alternative Title: None

Directed By: Jerry Schatzberg

Produced By: Dominick Dunne

Written By: Joan Didion

Color: Color

Length: 110 minutes

Language: English

Production Company: Didion-Dunne Inc.

Cast: Al Pacino, Kitty Winn, Alan Vint, Richard Bright, Kiel Martin, Michael McClanathan, Warren Finnerty, Marcia Jean Kurtz, and Raul Julia

Film Synopsis

The Panic in Needle Park portrays the life of heroin addicts who hang out at Needle Park (Sherman Square) in New York City. The film focuses on the story of two lovers, Bobby (Al Pacino) and Helen (Kitty Winn), and their relationship and addiction to heroin. The film was adapted for the screen from the 1966 book, *The Panic in Needle Park* by James Mills.

AIDS

AIDS (acquired immune deficiency syndrome) is the manifestation of human immunodeficiency virus in the form of actual illness. According to UNAIDS over 38.6 million people are infected with HIV/AIDS. However, AIDS awareness among the populous is low. The film industry has provided many films that depict AIDS and AIDS/HIV-related issues. Although most of the films depicting AIDS are centered on homosexuals, there are films that focus on nonhomosexual victims such as *Common Threads: Stories from the Quilt* (1989). Films relevant to this topic can often pertain to other social issues, like homosexuality and death. AIDS is categorized as an individual issue because of its breadth and relevance to today's society.

Other films dealing with AIDS not detailed in this volume include: *Citizen Cohn* (1992), *Common Threads: Stories from the Quilt* (1989), *The Cure* (1995), *Dear Francis* (2005), *Ending AIDS: The Search for a Vaccine* (2005), *Kids* (1995), *Lifecycles: A Story of AIDS in Malawi* (2003), *The Living End* (1992), *Longtime Companion* (1990), *The Origins of AIDS* (2003), *Parting Glances* (1986), *The Ryan White Story* (1989), *Undetectable* (2001), *Voices from the Front* (1992), and *Walking on Water* (2002).

AN EARLY FROST

(1985)

Genre: Drama

MPAA Rating: Not Rated

Alternative Title: None

Directed By: John Erman

Produced By: Perry Lafferty

Written By: Ron Cowen, Daniel Lipman, and Sherman Yellen

Color: Color

Length: 97 minutes

Language: English

Production Company: NBC Productions

Cast: Gena Rowlands, Ben Gazzara, Sylvia Sidney, Aidan Quinn, D.W. Moffett, Christopher Bradley, and Bill Paxton

Film Synopsis

An Early Frost is a made-for-television film about a family dealing with a homosexual son who is dying from AIDS. Michael Pierson (Aidan Quinn) is a young lawyer who is homosexual. His family is unaware of his lifestyle until Michael becomes infected with AIDS. The family reacts unpredictably and life for Michael is not easy. He searches for support and eventually his family comes to his side. *An Early Frost* was nominated for a total of 14 Emmy Awards, for which it won four, including Outstanding Writing, and was nominated for three Golden Globe Awards, for which it won for Best Supporting Actress (Sylvia Sidney).

AND THE BAND PLAYED ON

(1993)

Genre: Drama

MPAA Rating: PG-13

Alternative Title: None

Directed By: Roger Spottiswoode

Produced By: Sarah Pillsbury and Midge Sanford

Written By: Arnold Schulman

Color: Color

Length: 141 minutes

Language: English

Production Company: Home Box Office/Odyssey Motion Pictures

Cast: Matthew Modine, Lily Tomlin, Glenne Headly, Alan Alda,
    Ian McKellan, Richard Gere, Steve Martin, and Ronald Guttman

Film Synopsis

And the Band Played On is a made-for-television film that traces the discovery of the AIDS epidemic and the political infighting of the scientific community hampering its prevention and possible cure. Dr. Don Francis (Matthew Modine), a scientist working at the Centers for Disease Control (CDC) in Atlanta, is researching the characteristics of a new disease dubbed the "gay cancer" among the gay community. The disease is ignored by the masses until infected individuals from outside the gay community emerge. *And the Band Played On* was adapted from the book *And the Band Played On: Politics, People, and the AIDS Epidemic* by Randy Shilts. The film was nominated for a total of 14 Emmy Awards, in which it won three, including Outstanding Made for Television Movie.

THE GIFT

(2003)

Genre: Documentary

MPAA Rating: Not Rated

Alternative Title: None

Directed By: Louise Hogarth

Produced By: Louise Hogarth

Written By: Louise Hogarth

Color: Color

Length: 62 minutes

Language: English

Production Company: Dream Out Loud Productions

Cast: Doug Hitzel

Film Synopsis

The Gift documents the phenomenon of deliberate HIV/AIDS infection. Seeking "the gift," or HIV/AIDS infection, is commonly referred to as "bug chasing." The documentary follows two bug chasers searching for someone to infect them. Those willing to infect others are commonly referred to as "gift givers." The film explores the glamorization of HIV/AIDS and the division it causes in the gay community. Furthermore, the film includes interviews and discussions with bug chasers, AIDS activists, noninfected men, and infected men.

PHILADELPHIA

(1993)

Genre: Drama

MPAA Rating: PG-13

Alternative Title: *At Risk*

Directed By: Jonathan Demme

Produced By: Jonathan Demme and Edward Saxon

Written By: Ron Nyswaner

Color: Color

Length: 125 minutes

Language: English

Production Company: TriStar Pictures

Cast: Tom Hanks, Denzel Washington, Jason Robards, Antonio Banderas, and Mary Steenburgen

Film Synopsis

Philadelphia is the story of Andrew Beckett (Tom Hanks), a gay lawyer infected with AIDS. Although Andrew is an outstanding lawyer, he is fired because of his disease. Andrew hires Joe Miller (Denzel Washington), a homophobic lawyer, to help him sue his former employer. Over the course of the trial, Joe makes a drastic transformation as he comes to appreciate Andrew for the person he is, seeing past his own prejudice. *Philadelphia* was nominated for five Academy Awards, for which it won two, Best Actor (Tom Hanks) and Best Song (*Streets of Philadelphia* by Bruce Springsteen).

RENT

(2005)

Genre: Musical/Drama

MPAA Rating: PG-13

Alternative Title: None

Directed By: Chris Columbus

Produced By: Chris Columbus, Michael Barnathan, and Robert De Niro

Written By: Stephen Chbosky

Color: Color

Length: 135 minutes

Language: English

Company: Rent Production LLC

Cast: Jesse L. Martin, Taye Diggs, Rosario Dawson, Adam Pascal, Anthony Rapp, and Tracie Thoms

Film Synopsis

RENT is a rock opera set in the East Village of New York City, spanning the course of 1 year. The film follows a close group of Bohemians through life as they deal with love, loss, addiction, and AIDS. *RENT* is based on Giacomo Puccini's Pulitzer Prize–winning Broadway play, "La Boheme."

ROCK HUDSON

(1990)

Genre: Biography/Drama

MPAA Rating: PG-13

Alternative Title: None

Directed By: John Nicolella

Produced By: Diana Kerew and Renee Palyo

Written By: Dennis Turner

Color: Color

Length: 100 minutes

Language: English

Company: Konigsberg International

Cast: Thomas Ian Griffith, Daphne Ashbrook, William R. Moses, Michael Ensign, and Andrew Robinson

Film Synopsis

Rock Hudson is a biography about film and television star Rock Hudson, who was one of the first famous personalities to be infected with AIDS. The film portrays Rock Hudson's homosexuality, struggles with AIDS, and other secrets. The film details Rock Hudson's divorce from Phyllis Gates and his discovery of being infected with AIDS and how he handles it. It also details the landmark case in which Marc Christian won against Hudson's estate, because Hudson did not inform his lover that he was infected with AIDS. The film is based on the book, *My Husband, Rock Hudson*, by Rock Hudson's ex-wife, Phyllis Gates.

Animal Rights

Animal rights is a social issue that has recently received more attention by the media and lawmakers. Many countries have implemented various animal rights laws that protect animals from some types of human exploitation. Animal rights issues are most notably associated with People for Ethical Treatment of Animals (PETA). Animal rights issues are also easily associated with the ramped popularity of dog fighting. However, animal rights issues are larger than that. Animal rights advocates approach the issue believing that all animals should no longer be regarded as property, used as food, clothing, research subjects, and/or for entertainment.

Other films dealing with animal rights not detailed in this volume include: *Born Free* (1966), *Casuistry: The Art of Killing a Cat* (2004), *Dealing Dogs: The Betrayal of Man's Best Friend* (2006), *Delicacy of Despair* (2003), *Endangered Mermaids: The Manatees of Florida* (2003), *Free Willy* (1993), *Free Willy 2: The Adventure Home* (1995), *Free Willy 3: The Rescue* (1997), *Grizzly Man* (2005), *Hoot* (2006), *Legally Blonde 2: Red, White, & Blonde* (2003), *Meet Your Meat* (2003), *The Shaggy Dog* (2006), *The Story of the Weeping Camel* (2003), *To Walk with Lions* (1999), and *Twelve Monkeys* (1995).

THE ANIMALS FILM

(1981)

Genre: Documentary

MPAA Rating: Not Rated

Alternative Title: None

Directed By: Myrium Alaux and Victor Schonfeld

Produced By: Myrium Alaux and Victor Schonfeld

Written By: Victor Schonfeld

Color: Color

Length: 136 minutes

Language: English

Production Company: Beyond the Frame

Cast: Julie Christie (narrator) and Sandy Dennis

Film Synopsis

The Animals Film is a documentary that explores and examines various types of animal abuse. The film depicts how animals are used as pets, entertainment, food, and research subjects. The film is narrated by Julie Christie and includes an array of footage, including government film clips and newsreels.

EARTHLINGS

(2003)

Genre: Documentary

MPAA Rating: PG

Alternative Title: None

Directed By: Shaun Monson

Produced By: Shaun Monson, Nicole Visram, Brett Harrelson, and Persia White

Written By: Shaun Monson

Color: Color/Black and white

Length: 95 minutes

Language: English

Production Company: Nation Earth

Cast: Joaquin Phoenix (narrator)

Film Synopsis

Earthlings is a documentary, narrated by Joaquin Phoenix, which chronicles the abuse of animals. The film examines how animals are used as pets, entertainment, food, and research subjects. The film also focuses on how many of the world's largest industries profit from animals. *Earthlings* includes various types of footage and an original score by Moby.

FAST FOOD NATION

(2006)

Genre: Drama

MPAA Rating: R

Alternative Title: None

Directed By: Richard Linklater

Produced By: Chris Salvaterra, Edward Saxon, Eric Schlosser, Jeff Skoll, Ricky Strauss, David M. Thompson, and Peter Watson

Written By: Eric Schlosser and Richard Linklater

Color: Color

Length: 116 minutes

Language: English

Production Company: BBC Films

Cast: Greg Kinnear, Wilmer Valderrama, Patricia Arquette, Ashley Johnson, Kris Kristofferson, Bruce Willis, Ethan Hawke, Avril Lavigne, and Luis Guzman

Film Synopsis

Fast Food Nation tells the story of Don Anderson (Greg Kinnear), the vice president of marketing for a fast food chain, and his investigation into how and why the company's hamburgers are tainted with bovine fecal matter. The film is loosely based on the book *Fast Food Nation: The Dark Side of the All-American Meal* by Eric Schlosser.

GORILLAS IN THE MIST: THE STORY OF DIAN FOSSEY

(1988)

Genre: Drama

MPAA Rating: PG-13

Alternative Title: *Gorillas in the Mist*

Directed By: Michael Apted

Produced By: Peter Gruber, Rick Baker, Terrance Clegg, Arne Glimcher, Judy Kessler, Jon Peters, and Robert Nixon

Written By: Anna Hamilton Phelan

Color: Color

Length: 129 minutes

Language: English

Production Company: The Guber-Peters Company

Cast: Sigourney Weaver, Bryan Brown, Julie Harris, Ian Glen,
David Lansbury, and Michael J. Reynolds

Film Synopsis

Gorillas in the Mist: The Story of Dian Fossey tells the true story of Dian Fossey, a scientist who spent her life studying and protecting endangered mountain gorillas in Rwanda. The film portrays the life, work, and sacrifices of Dian Fossey (Sigourney Weaver). The movie depicts Fossey's relationship with the gorillas, her failed romance with *National Geographic* photographer Bob Campbell (Bryan Brown), her advocate for protection of the gorillas from poachers, and her mysterious murder in 1985.

I AM AN ANIMAL: THE STORY OF INGRID NEWKIRK AND PETA

(2007)

Genre: Documentary

MPAA Rating: Not Rated

Alternative Title: None

Directed By: Matthew Galkin

Produced By: Mikaela Beardsley, Steven Cantor, Matthew Galkin,
and Pax Wassermann

Written By: None credited

Color: Color

Length: 72 minutes

Language: English

Production Company: Stick Figure Productions

Cast: Bill Maher, Ingrid Newkirk, Alex Pacheco, and Pink

Film Synopsis

I Am an Animal: The Story of Ingrid Newkirk and PETA is a documentary film that examines the beliefs, ideas, motives, and life of Ingrid Newkirk. Newkirk is a British-born animal rights activist who co-founded People for the Ethical Treatment of Animals (PETA), the world's largest animal rights organization.

YOUR MOMMY KILLS ANIMALS

(2007)

Genre: Documentary

MPAA Rating: R

Alternative Title: N/A

Directed By: Curt Johnson

Produced By: Curt Johnson, Maura Flynn, Earl Easley, and Dennis Banks

Written By: None credited

Color: Color

Length: 105 minutes

Language: English

Production Company: Indie Genius Productions

Cast: Ron Arnold, Jessica Biel, Cal Bryant, Sally Burns, Shane Barbi, James Cromwell, Sia Barbi, Bo Derek, Leo Grillo, Mark McGrath, and Ben Stein

Film Synopsis

Your Mommy Kills Animals is a documentary film that examines and explores the animal liberation movement in the United States. The film chronicles the conflicts between animal right activists and researchers, food companies, and others. The film also explores the Federal Bureau of Investigation's ranking of animal rights activists as the United States number one domestic terrorist threat.

Capital Punishment

Capital punishment, or the death penalty, is a popular social issue among the populous. Capital punishment is simply the practice of executing a human as punishment for a crime. Like many social issues, capital punishment is a common topic during elections of government officials and among religious groups. Films relevant to this topic can often pertain to other social issues, like death and the role of government. However, these social issues are handled separately in this chapter.

Other films dealing with capital punishment not detailed in this volume include: *Beyond a Reasonable Doubt* (1956), *Capote* (2005), *Cell 2455 Death Row* (1955), *Compulsion* (1959), *Execution* (2006), *The Execution of Raymond Graham* (1985), *The Executioner's Song* (1982), *The Exonerated* (2005), *Fighting for Life in the Death-Belt* (2005), *Fourteen Days in May* (1988), *I Want To Live* (1958), *Infamous* (2006), *Kill Me if You Can* (1977), *Last Dance* (1996), *Last Light* (1993), *A Lesson Before Dying* (1999), *Live! From Death Row* (1992), *Lost Behind Bars* (2006), *Monster's Ball* (2002), *One on Top of the Other* (1971), *A Short Film about Killing* (1987), *Thanatos Rx: The Death Penalty Debate in America* (2001), *Too Young to Die?* (1990), *True Crime* (1999), *The Verdict* (1946), and *Witness to the Execution* (1994).

10 RILLINGTON PLACE

(1971)

Genre: Crime, Drama

MPAA Rating: PG

Alternative Title: None

Directed By: Richard Fleischer

Produced By: Leslie Linder and Martin Ransohoff

Written By: Clive Exton

Color: Color

Length: 111 minutes

Language: English

Production Company: Filmways Pictures

Cast: Richard Attenborough, Judy Geeson, John Hurt, Pat Heywood, Isobel Black, Miss Riley, Phyllis MacMahon, and Ray Barron

Film Synopsis

10 Rillington Place is based on a true story of John Reginald Halliday Christie, a British serial killer who raped and killed women in the 1940s and 1950s. Christie (Richard Attenborough) persuades Tim Evans (John Hurt) and his wife Beryl (Judy Geeson) into allowing him to perform an illegal abortion on Beryl. However, Christie instead rapes and kills Beryl and the baby and frames Tim for the crime. Tim is then arrested, tried, and convicted of murder and sentenced to death. *10 Rillington Place* was adapted from Ludovic Kennedy's book, *Ten Rillington Place*.

DEAD MAN WALKING

(1995)

Genre: Drama

MPAA Rating: R

Alternative Title: None

Directed By: Tim Robbins

Produced By: Jon Kilik, Tim Robbins, and Rudd Simmons

Written By: Tim Robbins

Color: Color

Length: 122 minutes

Language: English

Production Company: Havoc

Cast: Susan Sarandon, Sean Penn, Robert Prosky, Raymond J. Barry, Kevin Cooney, Scott Wilson, Roberta Maxwell, and Nesbitt Blaisdell

Film Synopsis

Dead Man Walking is based on true events and tells the story of a nun and her relationship with a convicted murderer. Sister Helen Prejean (Susan Sarandon) builds a relationship with Matthew Poncelet (Sean Penn) as his execution date moves near. *Dead Man Walking* is based on the nonfiction book by the same name written by Sister Helen Prejean. The film was nominated for four Academy Awards, in which it won Best Actress in a Leading Role (Susan Sarandon).

DEADLINE

(2004)

Genre: Documentary

MPAA Rating: R

Alternative Title: *Life after Death Row*

Directed By: Katy Chevigny and Kirsten Johnson

Produced By: Katy Chevigny and Dallas Brennan

Written By: None Credited

Color: Color

Length: 90 minutes

Language: English

Production Company: Arts Engine

Cast: Anthony Amsterdam, Stephen Bright, Donald Cabana,
    Tom Cross, Gary Gauger, Cornelia Grumman, Elaine Jones,
    and Larry Marshall

Film Synopsis

Deadline is an award-winning documentary that examines capital punishment in the United States. The film's central focus is on the actions of the Governor of Illinois, George H. Ryan, and his historic decision to commute 167 inmates' death sentences to life without parole. Governor Ryan's awareness of possible flaws in the American justice system and sentencing of innocent citizens to death helped him make the historic decision.

THE GREEN MILE

(1999)

MPAA Rating: R

Alternative Title: *Stephen King's The Green Mile*

Directed By: Frank Darabont

Produced By: Frank Darabont and David Valdes

Written By: Frank Darabont

Color: Color

Length: 188 minutes

Language: English

Production Company: Castle Rock Entertainment

Cast: Tom Hanks, David Morse, Bonnie Hunt, Michael Clarke Duncan,
    Barry Pepper, Graham Greene, Doug Hutchison, Jeffrey DeMunn,
    and Patricia Clarkson

Film Synopsis

The Green Mile tells the story of Paul Edgecomb (Tom Hanks) and his life as a death row corrections officer in the 1930s. The film highlights various events surrounding the relationship and execution of death row prisoners that ultimately impacts Edgecomb's perspective on his life and job. *The Green Mile* was based on Stephen King's novel by the same name. The film was nominated for four Academy Awards including Best Picture and Best Supporting Actor.

IN COLD BLOOD

(1967)

Genre: Crime/Drama

MPAA Rating: R

Alternative Title: *Truman Capote's In Cold Blood*

Directed By: Richard Brooks

Produced By: Richard Brooks

Written By: Richard Brooks

Color: Black and White

Length: 134 minutes

Language: English

Production Company: Columbia Pictures Corporation

Cast: Robert Blake, Scott Wilson, John Forsythe, Paul Stewart, Gerald S. O'Loughlin, Jeff Corey, John Gallaudet, James Flavin, and Charles McGraw

Film Synopsis

In Cold Blood is based on true events and was adapted for the screen from Truman Capote's book by the same name. The film depicts the criminal investigation, trial, and execution of Perry Smith (Robert Blake) and Richard Hickock (Scott Wilson), who in 1959 murder Herbert Clutter and his wife and two children. *In Cold Blood* was nominated for four Academy Awards including Best Director and Best Screenplay.

THE LIFE OF DAVID GALE

(2003)

Genre: Drama

MPAA Rating: R

Alternative Title: None

Directed By: Alan Parker

Produced By: Nicolas Cage and Alan Parker

Written By: Charles Randolph

Color: Color

Length: 130 minutes

Language: English

Production Company: Universal Pictures

Cast: Kate Winslet, Cleo King, Constance Jones, Kevin Spacey,
Laura Linney, Lee Ritchey, Gabriel Mann, Matt Craven,
Brandy Little, and Leon Rippy

Film Synopsis

The Life of David Gale tells the story of David Gale (Kevin Spacey), a
university professor and active opponent of capital punishment. Gale loses
his job because he is accused of raping a student and is then convicted
of murdering his colleague, Constance Harraway (Laura Linney), and is
sentenced to death. Prior to the execution, a journalist named Bitsy Bloom
(Kate Winslet) interviews David Gale and starts to uncover clues that point
to Gale's innocence.

Censorship

Censorship has been portrayed on the big screen in various ways
throughout cinematic history. Simply put, censorship is the suppression or
deletion of ideas and information that is considered to be objectionable or
dangerous. Censorship's depiction on film has included social/moral, religious, political, corporate, and military types of censorship. Films relevant
to censorship can often pertain to other social issues, such as media and the
role of government. However, these social issues are handled separately in
this chapter.

Other films dealing with censorship not detailed in this volume include:
-30- (1959), *Cartoon Crazys Banned and Censored* (2000), *Censor* (2001), *The
Chatterley Affair* (2006), *Cradle Will Rock* (1999), *Damned in the U.S.A.* (1991),
Dirty Pictures (2000), *Empire of Censors* (1995), *Expelled: No Intelligence Allowed*
(2008), *Fear, Panic, & Censorship* (2000), *Forbidden Under the Censorship of the
King* (1972), *The Front* (1976), *The Insider* (1999), *Iraq: A Tale of Censorship*
(2007), *Lenny Bruce: Without Tears* (1972), *The Notorious Betty Page* (2005),
One Nation Under (2005), *Park Row* (1952), *The People vs. Larry Flint* (1996),
Pleasantville (1998), *Priest of Love* (1981), *Private Parts* (1997), *Sex, Censor-
ship and the Silver Screen* (1996), and *Smothered: The Censorship Struggles of the
Smothers Brothers Comedy Hour* (2002).

GOOD MORNING, VIETNAM

(1987)

Genre: Comedy/Drama

MPAA Rating: R

Alternative Title: None

Directed By: Barry Levinson

Produced By: Larry Brezner and Mark Johnson

Written By: Mitch Markowitz

Color: Color

Length: 121 minutes

Language: English

Production Company: Touchstone Pictures

Cast: Robin Williams, Forest Whitaker, Tung Thanh Tran,
   J.T. Walsh, Chintara Sukapatana, Bruno Kirby, Richard Portnow,
   Dan Stanton, and Noble Willingham

Film Synopsis

Good Morning, Vietnam is loosely based on the true story of Adrian Cronauer. The film is set in Saigon during the Vietnam War and tells the story of Adrian Cronauer (Robin Williams), an Armed Forces Radio disc jockey and his original, humorous, and sometimes controversial radio broadcasts. The film was nominated for an Academy Award for Best Actor (Robin Williams) and won a Golden Globe for Best Actor (Robin Williams).

INHERIT THE WIND

(1960)

Genre: Drama

MPAA Rating: PG

Alternative Title: None

Directed By: Stanley Kramer

Produced By: Stanley Kramer

Written By: Nedrick Young

Color: Black and white

Length: 128 minutes

Language: English

Production Company: Stanley Kramer Productions

Cast: Spencer Tracy, Fredric March, Gene Kelly, Dick York,
    Donna Anderson, Harry Morgan, Claude Akins, Elliott Reid,
    Paul Hartman, Jimmy Boyd, and Gordon Polk

Film Synopsis

Inherit the Wind is based on the true story of John T. Scopes and the 1925 Scopes Monkey Trial. The film depicts the criminal trial and conviction of Bertram Cates (Dick York), who was charged for teaching his high school science class about Charles Darwin's theory of evolution. *Inherit the Wind* was nominated for four Academy Awards including Best Actor and Best Screenplay.

LENNY

(1974)

Genre: Biography

MPAA Rating: R

Alternative Title: None

Directed By: Bob Fosse

Produced By: Marvin Worth

Written By: Julian Barry

Color: Black and white

Length: 111 minutes

Language: English

Production Company: Marvin Worth Productions

Cast: Dustin Hoffman, Valerie Perrine, Stanley Beck, Jan Miner,
    Frankie Man, Rashel Novikoff, Gary Morton, Guy Rennie,
    and Kathryn Witt

Film Synopsis

Lenny is a biographical account based on the play by Julian Barry and tells the story of Lenny Bruce (Dustin Hoffman) and his controversial comedy act. The film details Bruce's life from his early career to his death in 1966. *Lenny* was nominated for six Academy Awards including Best Actor and Best Picture.

PUMP UP THE VOLUME

(1990)

Genre: Drama

MPAA Rating: R

Alternative Title: None

Directed By: Allan Moyle

Produced By: Rupert Harvey and Sandy Stern

Written By: Allan Moyle

Color: Color

Length: 102 minutes

Language: English

Production Company: New Line Cinema

Cast: Christian Slater, Annie Ross, Andy Romano, Mimi Kennedy, Scott Paulin, Ellen Greene, Anthony Lucero, Billy Morrissette, Robert Schenkkan, and Seth Green

Film Synopsis

Pump up the Volume tells the story of Mark Hunter (Christian Slater) and his controversial radio show. Mark is a shy teenager who hosts a pirated radio show under the name Hard Harry. Hard Harry's controversial radio broadcasts cause the local teenagers to speak out and the community to panic.

STORM CENTER

(1956)

Genre: Drama

MPAA Rating: Not Rated

Alternative Title: *The Library*

Directed By: Daniel Taradash

Produced By: Julian Blaustein

Written By: Elick Moll and Daniel Taradash

Color: Black and white

Length: 85 minutes

Language: English

Production Company: Julian Blaustein Productions Ltd.

Cast: Bette Davis, Brian Keith, Kim Hunter, Paul Kelly, Kevin Coughlin, Joe Mantell, Sally Brophy, Howard Wierum, Curtis Cooksey, and Edward Platt

Film Synopsis

Storm Center tells the story of a small-town librarian, Alicia Hull (Bette Davis). She is fired and branded as a communist when she refuses to remove a book titled *The Communists Dream* from the library's collection.

THIS FILM IS NOT YET RATED

(2006)

Genre: Documentary

MPAA Rating: Not Rated

Alternative Title: None

Directed By: Kirby Dick

Produced By: Eddie Schmidt

Written By: Eddie Schmidt and Kirby Dick

Color: Color

Length: 97 minutes

Language: English

Production Company: Independent Film Channel

Cast: Kimberly Peirce, Jon Lewis, David Ansen, Martin Garbus, Wayne Kramer, Kevin Smith, John Waters, Richard Heffner, and Matt Stone

Film Synopsis

This Film is Not Yet Rated is a documentary about the Motion Picture Association of America and its impact on cinema and culture. The film specifically examines and highlights the Motion Picture Association of America's film rating system and its inequities and biases.

Child Abuse

Child abuse is one social issue that the majority of the populous would agree on. However, what is not always agreed upon is the punishment for child abusers and more important, what constitutes child abuse. Child abuse is most often defined as the verbal, physical, emotional, psychological, and/or sexual maltreatment of a child. Child abuse has often been depicted on film and has become a more common aspect of films in the last 30–40 years. Films relevant to child abuse can often pertain to other social issues, such as divorce and spouse abuse. However, these social issues are handled separately in this chapter.

Other films depicting child abuse not detailed in this volume include: *Abuse* (1983), *Adam: His Song Continues* (1986), *Antwone Fisher* (2002), *Capturing the Friedmans* (2003), *Child of Rage* (1992), *The Children of Times Square* (1986), *Chinatown* (1974), *Deliver Us from Evil* (2006), *Do You Know the Muffin Man?* (1989), *Don't Touch My Daughter* (1991), *Fallen Angel* (1981), *Fiona* (1998), *Flowers in the Attic* (1987), *The Girl Next Door* (2007), *Happiness* (1998), *Hearts of the World* (1918), *I Know My First Name is Steven* (1989), *Karla* (2006), *Kids Don't Tell* (1985), *Little Boy Blue* (1997), *Little Children* (2006), *Martyrs* (2008), *Mary Jane Harper Cried Last Night* (1977), *Maya* (2001), *Missing Children: A Mother's Story* (1982), *Mommie Dearest* (1981), *Mystic River* (2003), *A Promise to Carolyn* (1996), *The Reader* (2008), *Return to Innocence* (2001), *Right to Kill?* (1985), *Shattered Trust: The Shari Karney Story* (1993), *Sling Blade* (1996), *Slumdog Millionaire* (2008), *Song for a Raggy Boy* (2003), *Sparrows* (1926), *This Boy's Life* (1993), *Unforgivable* (1996), *Unspeakable Acts* (1990), *While Justice Sleeps* (1994), and *Who'll Save the Children?* (1978).

AN AMERICAN CRIME

(2007)

Genre: Drama/Crime

MPAA Rating: R

Alternative Title: *The Basement*

Directed By: Tommy O'Haver

Produced By: Jocelyn Hayes, Katie Roumel, Kevin Turen, Christine Vachon, and Henry Winterstern

Written By: Tommy O'Haver and Irene Turner

Color: Color

Length: 97 minutes

Language: English

Production Company: First Look International

Cast: Ellen Page, Hayley McFarland, Nick Searcy, Romy Rosemont,
 Catherine Keener, Ari Graynor, Michael O'Keefe,
 Bradley Whitford, and Michelle Benes

Film Synopsis

An American Crime is based on the true story of Sylvia Likens, a teenage
girl who was tortured and murdered in the 1960s. The film tells the horrific story of Gertrude Baniszewski (Catherine Keener) and her role in the
events surrounding the abuse, torture, and eventual murder of Sylvia Likens (Ellen Page). Likens was locked in a basement and tortured by Baniszewski and others until she eventually died. The film portrays the abuse and
the criminal trial. *An American Crime* was nominated for an Emmy Award
and a Golden Globe for Best Actor (Catherine Keener).

INDICTMENT: THE McMARTIN TRIAL

(1995)

Genre: Drama

MPAA Rating: R

Alternative Title: None

Directed By: Mick Jackson

Produced By: Diana Pokorny

Written By: Abby Mann and Myra Mann

Color: Color

Length: 135 minutes

Language: English

Production Company: Abby Mann Productions

Cast: James Woods, Mercedes Ruehl, Lolita Davidovich,
 Sada Thompson, Henry Thomas, Shirley Knight, Mark Bloom,
 Alison Elliot, and Scott Armstrong

Film Synopsis

Indictment: The McMartin Trial is based on the true story of the McMartin family and the criminal trial surrounding the allegations of child molestation. The film tells the story of the McMartin family and how their lives
were forever changed because of allegations of child molestation. The film
specifically depicts the criminal trial of the McMartin family, which, after
6 years, millions of dollars, and the imprisonment of the accused, resulted

in a dismissal. *Indictment: The McMartin Trial* was nominated for eight Emmy Awards, in which it won three, including Best Television Movie. The film was also nominated for four Golden Globes, in which it won two, including Best Television Movie.

RADIO FLYER

(1993)

Genre: Drama

MPAA Rating: PG-13

Alternative Title: None

Directed By: Richard Donner

Produced By: Lauren Shuler Donner

Written By: David M. Evans

Color: Color

Length: 114 minutes

Language: English

Production Company: Columbia Pictures Corporation

Cast: Lorraine Bracco, John Heard, Tom Hanks, Adam Baldwin, Elijah Wood, Ben Johnson, Joseph Mazzello, Sean Baca, Garette Ratliff Henson, and Robert Munich

Film Synopsis

Radio Flyer depicts the events of two brothers in the 1960s and the abuse that one of them endures from their stepfather. The brothers, Mike (Elijah Wood) and Bobby (Joseph Mazzello), build an airplane using a radio flyer wagon, so that Bobby may escape from the abuse.

SLEEPERS

(1996)

Genre: Drama

MPAA Rating: R

Alternative Title: None

Directed By: Barry Levinson

Produced By: Barry Levinson and Steve Golin

Written By: Barry Levinson

Color: Black and white/Color

Length: 147 minutes

Language: English

Production Company: Baltimore Pictures

Cast: Kevin Bacon, Billy Crudup, Robert De Niro, Dustin Hoffman,
    Ron Eldard, Minnie Driver, Brad Renfro, Brad Pitt,
    and Vittorio Gassman

Film Synopsis

Sleepers tells the story of four teenage boys in Hell's Kitchen, New York,
who are sentenced to serve time in a boys' home upstate. Once there, the
four teenagers are beaten and raped by the guards. Years after the boys
are released, they seek revenge on the guards. *Sleepers* is based on the book
by Lorenzo Carcaterra by the same name. The film was nominated for an
Academy Award for Best Original Score.

SYBIL

(1976)

Genre: Drama

MPAA Rating: Not Rated

Alternative Title: None

Directed By: Daniel Petrie

Produced By: Jacqueline Babbin

Written By: Stewart Stern

Color: Color

Length: 198 minutes

Language: English

Production Company: Lorimar Productions

Cast: Joanne Woodward, Sally Field, Brad Davis, Martine Bartlett,
    Jane Hoffman, Charles Lane, Jessamine Milner, William Prince,
    and Penelope Allen

Film Synopsis

Sybil is a made-for-television film based on the true story of Shirley Mason.
The film depicts the life of Sybil (Sally Field) and her horrific childhood. As

a child, Sybil was psychologically and sexually abused, causing her to develop 13 different personalities. *Sybil* is based on the book by Flora Rheta Schreiber by the same name. It was nominated for six Emmy Awards, in which it won four, including Outstanding Drama and Outstanding Actress (Sally Field).

ULTIMATE BETRAYAL

(1994)

Genre: Drama

MPAA Rating: Not Rated

Alternative Title: None

Directed By: Donald Wrye

Produced By: Julian Marks

Written By: Gregory Goodell

Color: Color

Length: 96 minutes

Language: English

Production Company: Hearst Entertainment Productions

Cast: Marlo Thomas, Mel Harris, Eileen Heckart, Kathryn Dowling, Henry Czerny, Donna Goodhand, David B. Nichols, Justin Louis, and Joanne Vannicola

Film Synopsis

Ultimate Betrayal, based on a true story, tells the story of two daughters who sue their father for incest and child abuse. As the story progresses, it is revealed that the father sexually abused all four of his daughters and physically abused his two sons.

Consumerism

> *The only reason a great many American families don't own an elephant is that they have never been offered an elephant for a dollar down and easy weekly payments.*
>
> —*Mad* magazine

Consumerism is unique in the sense of how it has been depicted on film. However, throughout the history of film, consumerism has been portrayed, from the accumulation of material goods to exhausting the earth's natural resources. The films detailed in this section focus centrally on the collection or consumption of goods and the exploitation of people and/ or the environment for the development, marketing, and/or sale of goods. Films relevant to consumerism can pertain to other social issues, like labor practices. However, this social issue is handled separately in this chapter.

Other films dealing with consumerism not detailed in this volume include: *99 Francs* (2007), *American Psycho* (2000), *As Is: A Downsized Life* (2005), *Blood Diamond* (2006), *Consumerism! The Musical* (2007), *The End of Suburbia: Oil Depletion and the Collapse of the American Dream* (2004), *Envy* (2004), *Escape from Affluenza* (1998), *Everything's Gone Green* (2006), *Fight Club* (1999), *Going Shopping* (2005), *Gone Shopping* (2007), *How to Get Ahead in Advertising* (1989), *Idiocracy* (2006), *In Debt We Trust* (2006), *King Corn* (2007), *King Kong* (2005), *Maxed Out* (2005), *Mean Girls* (2004), *Mr. Deeds Goes to Town* (1936), *Over the Hedge* (2006), *Reverend Billy and the Church of Stop Shopping* (2002), *The Rocking Horse Winner* (1950), *The Stuff* (1985), *Surplus: Terrorized into Being Consumers* (2003), *Thank You for Smoking* (2005), *They Live* (1988), and *WALL-E* (2008).

CONFESSIONS OF A SHOPAHOLIC

(2009)

Genre: Comedy/Romance

MPAA Rating: PG

Alternative Title: None

Directed By: P.J. Hogan

Produced By: Jerry Bruckheimer

Written By: Tracey Jackson, Tim Firth, and Kayla Alpert

Color: Color

Length: N/A

Language: English

Production Company: Touchstone Pictures

Cast: Isla Fisher, Hugh Dancy, Krysten Ritter, Joan Cusack, John Goodman, and Nick Cornish

Film Synopsis

Confessions of a Shopaholic tells the story of Rebecca Bloomwood (Isla Fisher) who is the ultimate consumer. Rebecca has a shopping addiction and moves to Manhattan to support her love for shopping. Although she is heavily in debt, she continues to shop and attempts to find new ways to support her love for shopping. *Confessions of a Shopaholic* is based on the books, *Confessions of a Shopaholic* and *Shopaholic take Manhattan* written by Sophie Kinsella.

THE CORPORATION

(2003)

Genre: Documentary

MPAA Rating: Not Rated

Alternative Title: None

Directed By: Mark Achbar and Jennifer Abbott

Produced By: Mark Achbar and Bart Simpson

Written By: Joel Bakan

Color: Color

Length: 145 minutes

Language: English

Production Company: Big Picture Media Corporation

Cast: Jane Akre, Ray Anderson, Maude Barlow, Chris Barrett, Carlton Brown, Smedley Darlington Butler, Noam Chomsky, Samuel Epstein, and Michael Moore

Film Synopsis

The Corporation is a documentary film that examines and explores modern-day corporations. The film specifically examines the business practices of many corporations and their legal malfeasance. The film criticizes corporations for focusing only on profit gains and targeting consumers using deceitful tactics without regard for the consumer or guilt.

THE GIRL FROM MONDAY

(2005)

Genre: Action

MPAA Rating: R

Alternative Title: None

Directed By: Hal Hartley

Produced By: Steve Hamilton and Hal Hartley

Written By: Hal Hartley

Color: Black and white/Color

Length: 84 minutes

Language: English

Production Company: Possible Films

Cast: Bill Sage, Sabrina Lloyd, Tatiana Abracos, Leo Fitzpatrick, D.J. Mendel, James Urbaniak, Juliana Francis, Gary Wilmes, and David Neumann

Film Synopsis

The Girl from Monday tells the story of a futuristic society where the consumer is king. In this society all people are bar-coded on the wrist and are treated like a product. People are marketed, sold, and traded. However, some people do not agree with the capitalistic system and attempt to go against the grain, only to become enemies of the corporation.

WAL-MART: THE HIGH COST OF LOW PRICES

(2005)

Genre: Documentary

MPAA Rating: Not Rated

Alternative Title: None

Directed By: Robert Greenwald

Produced By: Jim Gilliam, Robert Greenwald, and Devin Smith

Written By: None credited

Color: Color

Length: 98 minutes

Language: English

Production Company: Brave New Films

Cast: Edith Arana, James Cromwell, Diane DeVoy, Jordan Esry, Red Esry, Scott Esry, Frances Fisher, Stan Fortune, Rev. James Lawson, and Sandra Laney

Film Synopsis

Wal-Mart: The High Cost of Low Prices is a documentary that explores the impact Wal-Mart has on local communities. The film examines various individuals from across the country and details how they are struggling to live in a Wal-Mart world.

WHAT WOULD JESUS BUY?

(2007)

Genre: Documentary

MPAA Rating: PG

Alternative Title: None

Directed By: Rob VanAlkemade

Produced By: Peter Hutchison, Stacey Offman, and Morgan Spurlock

Written By: None Credited

Color: Color

Length: 91 minutes

Language: English

Production Company: Warrior Poets

Cast: Bill Talen, Adetola Abiade, Paul Norman Allen, Shannon Baxter, Rick Becker, James Solomon Benn, Ben Cerf, and Leah Farrell

Film Synopsis

What Would Jesus Buy? is a documentary that examines the commercialization of Christmas in American culture and the overconsumption of material goods. The film follows Reverend Billy and his choir on a cross-country journey as they spread their message singing anti-consumer-related songs.

YOU CAN'T TAKE IT WITH YOU

(1938)

Genre: Comedy

MPAA Rating: Not Rated

Alternative Title: None

Directed By: Frank Capra

Produced By: Frank Capra

Written By: Robert Riskin

Color: Black and white

Length: 126 minutes

Language: English

Production Company: Columbia Pictures Corporation

Cast: Jean Arthur, James Stewart, Edward Arnold, Lionel Barrymore,
Ann Miller, Mischa Auer, Donald Meek, H.B. Warner,
and Dub Taylor

Film Synopsis

You Can't Take it With You tells the story of two families whose lifestyles
and social classes clash. Alice (Jean Arthur) is from a unique family and falls
in love with her boss, Tony (James Stewart), whose family is very wealthy and
powerful. After the families meet, the relationship ends, which causes some
changes in Tony's family. *You Can't Take it With You* was nominated for seven
Academy Awards, in which it won two for Best Picture and Best Director.
The film is based on the Pulitzer Prize–winning play by George S. Kaufman
and Moss Hart by the same name.

Death

Death is one of the most common and regular elements of movies.
Death is simply the end of life. However, death as a social issue is more
complex. The controversy surrounding death typically is associated with
euthanasia, right to die, and suicide. Films portraying these death related
issues will be detailed in this section, as well as films depicting terminally ill
individuals and their impact on friends and family. Films relevant to death
can often pertain to other social issues such as AIDS and religion. However,
these social issues are handled separately in this chapter.

Other films dealing with death not detailed in this volume include: *Act
of Love* (1980), *Alex: The Life of a Child* (1986), *The Altruist* (2004), *Anand*
(1971), *Dead Poets Society* (1989), *Dr. Cook's Garden* (1971), *In the Matter of
Karen Ann Quinlan* (1977), *Knockin' on Heaven's Door* (1997), *Last Holiday*
(2006), *Life as a House* (2001), *Mademoiselle and the Doctor* (2004), *Magnolia*
(1999), *Mar Adentro* (2004), *The Miracle of Kathy Miller* (1982), *Murder or
Mercy* (1974), *My Girl* (1991), *My Life Without Me* (2003), *Night Unto Night*
(1949), *Peaceful Exit* (1995), *Prescription: Suicide?* (2005), *Reversal of Fortune*
(1990), *Romeo + Juliet* (1996), *The Shawshank Redemption* (1994), *Slender
Thread* (1965), *The Time Being* (1998), *Time to Say Goodbye?* (1997), *Walking
on Water* (2002), *When the Time Comes* (1987), and *Wit* (2001).

AN ACT OF MURDER

(1948)

Genre: Drama

MPAA Rating: Not Rated

Alternative Title: *Live Today for Tomorrow*

Directed By: Michael Gordon

Produced By: Jerry Bresler

Written By: Michael Blankfort

Color: Black and white

Length: 91 minutes

Language: English

Production Company: Universal International Pictures

Cast: Fredric March, Edmond O'Brian, Florence Eldridge, Geraldine Brooks, Stanley Ridges, John McIntire, Frederic Tozere, and Will Wright

Film Synopsis

An Act of Murder tells the story of an iron-fisted judge (Fredric March) and his struggles with his terminally ill wife. Cooke's wife is diagnosed with brain cancer and as the disease progresses her suffering increases. Yearning to stop his wife's suffering, he considers killing her, but is conflicted about the moral and legal ramifications. The film was based on the novel, *The Mills of God*, by Ernst Lothar.

THE BUCKET LIST

(2007)

Genre: Adventure

MPAA Rating: PG-13

Alternative Title: None

Directed By: Rob Reiner

Produced By: Alan Greisman, Rob Reiner, Neil Meron, and Craig Zadan

Written By: Justin Zackham

Color: Color

Length: 97 minutes

Language: English

Production Company: Storyline Entertainment

Cast: Jack Nicholson, Morgan Freeman, Sean Hayes, Beverly Todd,
Rob Morrow, Alfonso Freeman, Angela Gardner,
and Ian Anthony Dale

Film Synopsis

The Bucket List tells the story of two terminally ill patients who decide to live the rest of their days to the fullest. Two strangers, Edward Cole (Jack Nicholson) and Carter Chambers (Morgan Freeman), with nothing in common except the fact they are both dying, travel the world attempting to complete a list of things that they have never done. The film's soundtrack was nominated for a Grammy Award for John Mayer's song "Say."

RIGHT OF WAY

(1983)

Genre: Drama

MPAA Rating: Not Rated

Alternative Title: None

Directed By: George Schaefer

Produced By: George Schaefer

Written By: Richard Less

Color: Color

Length: 102 minutes

Language: English

Production Company: HBO Premiere Films

Cast: Bette Davis, James Stewart, Melinda Dillon, Priscilla Morrill,
John Harkins, Jacque Lynn Colton, Louis Schaefer,
and Charles Walker

Film Synopsis

Right of Way is a made-for-television film that tells the story of an elderly couple and their battle to die on their own terms. Mini (Bette Davis) is diagnosed with a terminal illness and together Mini and her husband, Teddy (James Stewart), plan a joint suicide. However, the couple's daughter and others attempt to divert the couple's plan.

RIGHT TO DIE

(1987)

Genre: Drama

MPAA Rating: Not Rated

Alternative Title: None

Directed By: Paul Wendkos

Produced By: Karen Danaher-Dorr

Written By: Phil Penningroth

Color: Color

Length: 90 minutes

Language: English

Production Company: Ohlmeyer Communications Company

Cast: Raquel Welch, Michael Gross, Bonnie Bartlett, Peter Michael Goetz, Joanna Miles, Ed O'Neill, Diane Salinger, and Mark Shera

Film Synopsis

Right to Die is a made-for-television film that tells the story of a successful psychologist, Emily Bauer (Rachel Welch), who is diagnosed with Lou Gehrig's disease. As her disease progresses, Emily longs for death and pleads with her husband to help her die. *Right to Die* was nominated for three Emmy Awards and one Golden Globe for Best Actress (Rachel Welch).

THE VIRGIN SUICIDES

(1999)

Genre: Drama

MPAA Rating: R

Alternative Title: *Sofia Coppola's the Virgin Suicides*

Directed By: Sofia Coppola

Produced By: Francis Ford Coppola, Julie Costanzo, Dan Halsted, and Chris Hanley

Written By: Sofia Coppola

Color: Color

Length: 97 minutes

Language: English

Production Company: American Zoetrope

Cast: James Woods, Kathleen Turner, Josh Hartnett, Kirsten Dunst,
Scott Glenn, Danny DeVito, Hanna Hall, Chelse Swain,
and A.J. Cook

Film Synopsis

The Virgin Suicides is set in the suburbs of Detroit during the 1970s and
tells the story of five sisters who are sheltered by their overprotective parents.
The sisters, unhappy and wanting freedom, plan a group suicide. *The Virgin
Suicides* is based on the novel by the same name written by Jeffrey Eugenides.

WHOSE LIFE IS IT ANYWAY?

(1981)

Genre: Drama

MPAA Rating: R

Alternative Title: None

Directed By: John Badham

Produced By: Lawrence P. Bachmann

Written By: Brian Clark

Color: Color

Length: 105 minutes

Language: English

Production Company: Metro-Goldwyn-Mayer

Cast: Richard Dreyfuss, John Cassavetes, Christine Lahti, Bob Balaban,
Kenneth McMillan, Kaki Hunter, Thomas Carter, Alba Oms,
and Janet Eilber

Film Synopsis

Whose Life is it Anyway? tells the story of Ken Harrison (Richard Dreyfuss) who is paralyzed. The film depicts Ken's accident and his arguments
on whether he should be allowed to die. *Whose Life is it Anyway?* is based on
the 1972 television play by the same name.

Disabilities

Disabilities have regularly been portrayed on the big screen. Memo-
rable and award-winning depictions such as Dustin Hoffman as a savant in

Rain Man, Daniel Day-Lewis as a writer and painter with cerebral palsy in *My Left Foot,* or Jamie Fox as Ray Charles in *Ray.* The films detailed in the volume pertain to four disabilities: mental illness, mental handicaps, physical impairment, and visual/hearing impairment.

Other films dealing with mentally handicapped–related issues not detailed in this volume include: *Best Boy* (1979), *Bill: On His Own* (1983), *Forrest Gump* (1994), *Of Mice and Men* (1939), *Radio* (2003), *Rain Man* (1988), *Sling Blade* (1996), and *Walter and June* (1983).

Other films dealing with mental illness not detailed in this volume include: *Fight Club* (1999), *Manic* (2001), *One Flew Over the Cuckoo's Nest* (1975), *Proof* (2005), *The Snake Pit* (1948), *The Soloist* (2009), *Sybil* (1976), *Taxi Driver* (1976), and *Tender is the Night* (1962).

Other films dealing with physical impairment not detailed in this volume include: *Born on the Fourth of July* (1989), *Coming Home* (1978), *The Mighty* (1998), and *Rear Window* (1998).

Other films dealing with visual/hearing impairment not detailed in this volume include the following: *Black* (2005), *Mandy* (1952), *Mr. Holland's Opus* (1995), *Music Within* (2007), *Ray* (2004), *Scent of a Woman* (1992), *Sound and Fury* (2000), *Wildflower* (1991).

A BEAUTIFUL MIND

(2001)

Genre: Drama

MPAA Rating: PG-13

Alternative Title: None

Directed By: Ron Howard

Produced By: Brian Grazer and Ron Howard

Written By: Akiva Goldsman

Color: Color

Length: 135 minutes

Language: English

Production Company: Universal Pictures

Cast: Russell Crowe, Ed Harris, Jennifer Connelly, Christopher Plummer, Paul Bettany, Adam Goldberg, Josh Lucas, and Anthony Rapp

Film Synopsis

A Beautiful Mind is based on the life of John Nash, a brilliant mathematician. The film portrays the life of Nash (Russell Crowe) and chronicles his struggles with paranoid schizophrenia. *A Beautiful Mind* was inspired by Sylvia Nasar's bestselling book by the same name. The film was nominated for eight Academy Awards, in which it won Best Picture, Best Director, Best Supporting Actress (Jennifer Connelly), and Best Screenplay.

AS GOOD AS IT GETS

(1997)

Genre: Comedy

MPAA Rating: PG-13

Alternative Title: *Old Friends*

Directed By: James L. Brooks

Produced By: James L. Brooks, Bridget Johnson, and Kristi Zea

Written By: Mark Andrus

Color: Color

Length: 139 minutes

Language: English

Production Company: TriStar Pictures

Cast: Jack Nicholson, Helen Hunt, Greg Kinnear, Cuba Gooding Jr., Skeet Ulrich, Shirley Knight, and Yeardley Smith

Film Synopsis

As Good As It Gets tells the story of Melvin Udall (Jack Nicholson), a writer who suffers from a severe case of obsessive–compulsive disorder. Melvin's disorder and his dislike for others eventually are tested when he befriends a waitress named Carol Connelly (Helen Hunt) and a homosexual neighbor named Simon Bishop (Greg Kinnear). *As Good As It Gets* was nominated for seven Academy Awards, in which it won Best Actor (Jack Nicholson) and Best Actress (Helen Hunt).

BILL

(1981)

Genre: Drama

MPAA Rating: R

Alternative Title: None

Directed By: Anthony Page

Produced By: Mel Stuart

Written By: Corey Blechman

Color: Color

Length: 100 minutes

Language: English

Production Company: Alan Landsburg Productions

Cast: Mickey Rooney, Dennis Quaid, Largo Woodruff, Anna Maria Horsford, Harry Goz, Kathleen Maguire, William J. Daprato, and Raymond Serra

Film Synopsis

Bill is a made-for-television film that tells the true story of Bill Sackter. Bill (Mickey Rooney) is a mentally handicapped man who has been institutionalized since he was 7 years old. He is finally released and ventures into the world on his own. Bill eventually meets a nice family who welcomes him into their home. *Bill* was nominated for three Emmy Awards, in which it won two, including Best Actor (Mickey Rooney). *Bill* also won two Golden Globes for Best Made for Television Movie and Best Actor (Mickey Rooney).

I AM SAM

(2001)

Genre: Drama

MPAA Rating: PG-13

Alternative Title: None

Directed By: Jessie Nelson

Produced By: Jessie Nelson, Richard Solomon, Marshall Herskovitz, and Edward Zwick

Written By: Jessie Nelson and Kristine Johnson

Color: Color

Length: 132 minutes

Language: English

Production Company: New Line Cinema

Cast: Sean Penn, Michelle Pfeiffer, Dakota Fanning, Diane Wiest,
    Loretta Devine, Richard Schiff, Laura Dern, and Brad Silverman

Film Synopsis

I Am Sam tells the moving story of a mentally handicapped father and his relationship with his daughter. Sam (Sean Penn) has a daughter, Lucy (Dakota Fanning), but some people start to question Sam's ability to raise her. The issue is taken to court and Sam has to battle for custody. *I Am Sam* was nominated for an Academy Award for Best Actor (Sean Penn).

THE MIRACLE WORKER

(1962)

Genre: Drama

MPAA Rating: Not Rated

Alternative Title: None

Directed By: Arthur Penn

Produced By: Fred Coe

Written By: William Gibson

Color: Black and white

Length: 106 minutes

Language: English

Production Company: Playfilm Productions

Cast: Anne Bancroft, Victor Joy, Inga Swenson, Andrew Prine,
    Kathleen Comegys, Patty Duke, Diane Bryan, Donna Bryan,
    and Peggy Burke

Film Synopsis

The Miracle Worker is a biographical account of the life of Helen Keller. The film depicts the struggles and hardships of Helen Keller (Patty Duke) and her relationship with her teacher Annie Sullivan (Anne Bancroft). *The Miracle Worker* was based on Helen Keller's autobiography, *The Story of My Life*. The film was nominated for five Academy Awards, in which it won two for Best Actress (Anne Bancroft) and Best Supporting Actress (Patty Duke).

MY LEFT FOOT: THE STORY OF CHRISTY BROWN

(1989)

Genre: Drama

MPAA Rating: R

Alternative Title: None

Directed By: Jim Sheridan

Produced By: Noel Pearson

Written By: Shane Connaughton

Color: Color

Length: 103 minutes

Language: English

Production Company: Ferndale Films

Cast: Daniel Day-Lewis, Brenda Fricker, Alison Whelan, Kirsten Sheridan, Declan Croghan, Eanna MacLiam, and Marie Conmee

Film Synopsis

My Left Foot: The Story of Christy Brown is based on the true story of Christy Brown. The film chronicles the life of Brown (Daniel Day-Lewis), who was born with cerebral palsy and can only control his left foot. Despite his handicap, Christy grows up to become a writer and artist. *My Left Foot: The Story of Christy Brown* was based on Christy Brown's autobiography by the same name. The film was nominated for five Academy Awards, in which it won two for Best Actor (Daniel Day-Lewis) and Best Supporting Actress (Brenda Fricker).

Divorce

Divorce has been a prominent and often common aspect of movies. Simply put, divorce is the breakup of a marriage. Divorce has been depicted in all genres of film including comedies, romances, and dramas. Throughout cinematic history the depiction of divorce has changed with the views of society. Films relevant to divorce can often pertain to other social issues such as spousal abuse and women's rights. However, these social issues are handled separately in this chapter.

Other films dealing with divorce not detailed in this volume include: *Alimony* (1949), *The Bigamist* (1953), *A Bill of Divorcement* (1940), *Breaking Up is Hard To Do* (1979), *Children of Divorce* (1980), *Divorce American Style* (1968),

Divorce Iranian Style (1998), *The Divorce of Lady X* (1938), *Divorce Wars* (1982), *Dodsworth* (1936), *Domestic Disturbance* (2001), *Don't Change Your Husband* (1918), *Don't Divorce the Children* (1989), *How to Divorce Without Screwing Up Your Children* (2006), *Intolerable Cruelty* (2003), *Laws of Attraction* (2004), *The Marriage of a Young Stockbroker* (1971), *The Marrying Kind* (1952), *Must Love Dogs* (2005), *Old Wives for New* (1918), *The Parent Trap* (1998), *The Philadelphia Story* (1940), *Stepmom* (1998), *Under the Tuscan Sun* (2003), *The Unfaithful* (1947), and *Why Change Your Wife* (1920).

DIVORCE HIS – DIVORCE HERS

(1973)

Genre: Drama

MPAA Rating: Not Rated

Alternative Title: None

Directed By: Waris Hussein

Produced By: Terence Baker and Gareth Wigan

Written By: John Hopkins

Color: Color

Length: 180 minutes

Language: English

Production Company: World Film Services

Cast: Richard Burton, Elizabeth Taylor, Carrie Nye, Barry Foster, Gabriele Ferzetti, Daniela Surina, Thomas Baptiste, and Ronald Radd

Film Synopsis

Divorce His–Divorce Hers is a two-part film that depicts the dissolution of a marriage of 18 years, from each spouse's perspective. Part one tells the story from Martin Reynolds's (Richard Burton) point of view and part two tells the story from Jane Reynolds's (Elizabeth Taylor) point of view.

THE DIVORCEE

(1930)

Genre: Drama

MPAA Rating: Not Rated

Alternative Title: None

Directed By: Robert Z. Leonard

Produced By: Robert Z. Leonard

Written By: Nick Grinde, Zelda Sears, and John Meehan

Color: Color

Length: 82 minutes

Language: English

Production Company: Metro-Goldwyn-Mayer

Cast: Norma Shearer, Chester Morris, Conrad Nagel,
     Robert Montgomery, Florence Eldridge, Helene Millard,
     and Robert Elliot

Film Synopsis

The Divorcee portrays the difficulty of marriage. The film tells the story of Ted Martin (Chester Morris) and his marriage to Jerry Bernard (Norma Shearer). The couple's marriage falls apart because of infidelity on both sides. *The Divorcee* is based on the book by Ursula Parrott, *Ex-Wife*. The film was nominated for four Academy Awards, in which it won one for Best Actress (Norma Shearer).

THE FIRST WIVES CLUB

(1996)

Genre: Comedy

MPAA Rating: PG

Alternative Title: None

Directed By: Hugh Wilson

Produced By: Scott Rudin

Written By: Robert Harling

Color: Color

Length: 103 minutes

Language: English

Production Company: Paramount Pictures

Cast: Bette Midler, Goldie Hawn, Diane Keaton, Maggie Smith,
     Dan Hedaya, Sarah Jessica Parker, Stephen Collins,
     and Elizabeth Berkley

Film Synopsis

The First Wives Club tells the story of three divorced women who plan to get revenge on each of their ex-husbands. The trio, Elise (Goldie Hawn), Annie (Diane Keaton), and Brenda (Bette Midler), decide to hurt their husbands' financial well-being, since they helped their husbands obtain their financial success. *The First Wives Club* is based on the book by the same name by Olivia Goldsmith. The film was nominated for an Academy Award for Best Music.

KRAMER VS. KRAMER

(1979)

Genre: Drama

MPAA Rating: PG

Alternative Title: None

Directed By: Robert Benton

Produced By: Stanley R. Jaffe

Written By: Robert Benton

Color: Color

Length: 105 minutes

Language: English

Production Company: Columbia Pictures Corporation

Cast: Dustin Hoffman, Meryl Streep, Jane Alexander, Justin Henry, Howard Duff, George Coe, JoBeth Williams, Bill Moor, and Howland Chamberlain

Film Synopsis

Kramer vs. Kramer depicts the impact a couple's divorce has on all involved parties. Joanna (Meryl Streep) leaves her husband, Ted (Dustin Hoffman), and he is left to raise their son Billy (Justin Henry). Over a year later Joanna returns and wants her son, but Ted is not willing to hand over custody and a custody hearing follows. *Kramer vs. Kramer* is based on the novel by the same name written by Avery Corman. The film was nominated for nine Academy Awards, in which it won five, including Best Picture, Best Director, Best Actor (Dustin Hoffman), and Best Supporting Actress (Meryl Streep).

MRS. DOUBTFIRE

(1993)

Genre: Comedy

MPAA Rating: PG-13

Alternative Title: None

Directed By: Chris Columbus

Produced By: Mark Radcliffe, Robin Williams,
    and Marsha Garces Williams

Written By: Randi Mayem Singer

Color: Color

Length: 125 minutes

Language: English

Production Company: Blue Wolf

Cast: Robin Williams, Sally Field, Pierce Brosnan, Harvey Fierstein,
    Polly Holiday, Matthew Lawrence, and Mara Wilson

Film Synopsis

Mrs. Doubtfire is about a divorced father, Daniel Hillard (Robin Williams), who yearns to spend more time with his children who are in the custody of his ex-wife (Sally Field). Daniel secretly disguises himself as a female nanny and gets hired by his ex-wife to be the nanny of his children. *Mrs. Doubtfire* is based on the book, *Madame Doubtfire*, by Anne Fine. The film won an Academy Award for Best Makeup and two Golden Globes for Best Actor (Robin Williams) and Best Picture for a Comedy/Musical.

THE WAR OF THE ROSES

(1989)

Genre: Comedy

MPAA Rating: R

Alternative Title: None

Directed By: Danny DeVito

Produced By: James L. Brooks and Arnon Milchan

Written By: Michael Leeson

Color: Color

Length: 116 minutes

Language: English

Production Company: Gracie Films

Cast: Michael Douglas, Kathleen Turner, Danny DeVito,
Marianne Sägebrecht, Sean Astin, Heather Fairfield, Peter Donat,
and G.D. Spradlin

Film Synopsis

The War of the Roses depicts the story of Oliver Rose (Michael Douglas)
and Barbara Rose (Kathleen Turner), a wealthy couple who decide to get
a divorce. The film focuses on the couple's bitter divorce and battle for
material possessions, mainly the house. *The War of the Roses* is based on the
book by the same name by Warren Adler. The film was nominated for three
Golden Globes, including Best Picture.

Drugs

Drugs are simply a substance that alters or affects an individual's bodily
functions or mental state. Drugs are a common element of movies and have
been depicted in many ways, including the addiction to drugs, the selling/
distribution of drugs, and the impact drugs have on the individual and those
close to the individual. Drugs typically portrayed in films are marijuana, cocaine, crack, LSD, and heroin. Drugs as a social issue is more complex and this
section focuses on illegal drug trafficking and how the government attempts
to prevent the distribution and use of illegal drugs. Films relevant to drugs can
often pertain to other social issues such as addiction and role of government.
However, these social issues are handled separately in this chapter.

Other films dealing with drugs not detailed in this volume include: *Bad
Boys II* (2003), *The Border* (1982), *Grass* (1999), *Hempsters: Plant the Seed* (2008),
High: The True Tale of American Marijuana (2006), *Miami Vice* (2006), *New Jack
City* (1991), *Plan Colombia: Cash-In on the Drug War Failure* (2003), *Poppies are
Also Flowers* (1966), *Prince of Pot: The U.S. vs. Marc Emery* (2007), *The Salton
Sea* (2002), *Saving Grace* (2000), *Scarface* (1983), *Waiting to Inhale: Marijuana,
Medicine, and the Law* (2005), and *World's Most Dangerous Drug* (2006).

AMERICAN DRUG WAR: THE LAST WHITE HOPE

(2007)

Genre: Documentary

MPAA Rating: Not Rated

Alternative Title: None

Directed By: Kevin Booth

Produced By: Kevin Booth and George Booth

Written By: None Credited

Color: Color

Length: 120 minutes

Language: English

Production Company: Sacred Cow Productions

Cast: Joe Arpaio, Jello Biafra, Jeff Blackburn, Curt Booth,
Kevin Booth, Tommy Chong, Paris Chong, Judge James Gray,
and Gary Gardner

Film Synopsis

American Drug War: The Last White Hope is a documentary film about America's war on drugs. The film explores what is considered to be the United States' longest and most expensive war, through testimonials from those directly working or impacted by the war on drugs, including CIA agents, politicians, and gang members.

AMERICAN GANGSTER

(2007)

Genre: Crime

MPAA Rating: R

Alternative Title: *The Return of Superfly*

Directed By: Ridley Scott

Produced By: Brian Grazer and Ridley Scott

Written By: Steven Zaillian

Color: Color

Length: 157 minutes

Language: English

Production Company: Universal Pictures

Cast: Denzel Washington, Russell Crowe, Chiwetel Ejiofor, Josh Brolin,
Lymari Nadal, Ted Levine, Malcolm Goodwin, and Ruby Dee

Film Synopsis

American Gangster is based on the true story of Harlem gangster and drug smuggler Ray Lucas. The film tells the story of Ray Lucas (Denzel

Washington) and how he became one of the most powerful and influential drug dealers in America. The film chronicles Ray Lucas's life and the methods he used to smuggle drugs into the United States. *American Gangster* was nominated for two Academy Awards for Best Art Direction and Best Supporting Actress (Ruby Dee).

BLOW

(2001)

Genre: Biography

MPAA Rating: R

Alternative Title: None

Directed By: Ted Demme

Produced By: Ted Demme, Denis Leary, and Joel Stillerman

Written By: David McKenna

Color: Color

Length: 124 minutes

Language: English

Production Company: Apostle

Cast: Johnny Depp, Penélope Cruz, Franka Potente, Rachel Griffiths, Paul Reubens, Ray Liotta, Jesse James, and Kevin Gage

Film Synopsis

Blow focuses on the trafficking of illegal drugs into the United States and is based on the true story of George Jung. The film tells the story of Jung (Johnny Depp) and how he became an instrumental figure in the illegal trafficking of cocaine. *Blow* was adapted for the screen from Bruce Porter's book, *Blow: How a Small Town Boy Made $100 Million with the Medellin Cocaine Cartel and Lost It All.*

COCAINE COWBOYS

(2006)

Genre: Documentary

MPAA Rating: R

Alternative Title: None

Directed By: Billy Corben

Produced By: Billy Corben and Alfred Spellman

Written By: None credited

Color: Color

Length: 118 minutes

Language: English

Production Company: Rakontur

Cast: Jon Roberts, Al Sunshine, Sam Burstyn, Mickey Munday,
Bob Palumbo, Toni Mooney, Al Singleton, Edna Buchanan,
and Joseph Davis

Film Synopsis

Cocaine Cowboys is a documentary film that details the history of drug trafficking in America. The film specifically focuses on the illegal drug trade in Miami, Florida, during the 1970s and 1980s. The film includes interviews from law enforcement officers and organized crime affiliates. The film also includes actual news footage from the era.

MARIA FULL OF GRACE

(2004)

Genre: Drama

MPAA Rating: R

Alternative Title: *María llena eres de gracia*

Directed By: Joshua Marston

Produced By: Paul S. Mezey

Written By: Joshua Marston

Color: Color

Length: 101 minutes

Language: Spanish and English

Production Company: HBO Films

Cast: Catalina Sandino Moreno, Virginia Ariza, Yenny Paola Vega,
Rodrigo Sánchez Borhorquez, Wilson Guerrero,
and Charles Albert Patiño

Film Synopsis

Maria Full of Grace tells the story of Maria (Catalina Sandino Moreno), a 17-year-old Colombian teenager who needs to earn some money. Maria is offered a chance to earn some cash as a drug mule, and although she is pregnant she accepts the job. The film depicts the life of a drug mule, a common method of drug smuggling. The film was nominated for an Academy Award for Best Actress (Catalina Sandino Moreno).

TRAFFIC

(2000)

Genre: Crime

MPAA Rating: R

Alternative Title: *Traffik*

Directed By: Steven Soderbergh

Produced By: Laura Bickford, Edward Zwick, and Marshall Herskovitz

Written By: Stephen Gaghan

Color: Color

Length: 147 minutes

Language: English

Production Company: Bedford Falls Productions

Cast: Benicio Del Toro, Jacob Vargas, Andrew Chavez, Michael Saucedo, Tomas Milian, Michael Douglas, Russell G. Jones, Catherine Zeta-Jones, and Don Cheadle

Film Synopsis

Traffic depicts America's war on drugs through a series of interwoven stories. The film examines the illegal drug trade from the perspectives of a trafficker, politican, addict, and law enforcement officer. *Traffic* was adapted for the screen from the British Television series, *Traffik*. The film was nominated for five Academy Awards, in which it won four including Best Director and Best Supporting Actor (Benicio Del Toro).

Environmental Issues

Environmental issues are a uniquely depicted theme in many Hollywood films. Typically environmental issues are handled on the big screen as a futuristic result of the present-day misuses and abuses of the environment. End of the world–type movies and science fiction–related films are more commonly associated with environmental issues. Many consider global warming the only environmental issue. However, there are many other issues such as exploiting the world's natural resources and demolishing the rain forest. Films relevant to environmental issues can often pertain to other social issues such as consumerism. However, this social issue is handled separately in this chapter.

Other films dealing with environmental issues not detailed in this volume include: *Betrayed* (2003), *Blue Vinyl* (2002), *Can the Environment Get a Table Dance?* (2008), *Category 7: The End of the World* (2005), *Clear Cut: The Story of Philomath, Oregon* (2006), *Corn* (2004), *A Crude Awakening: The Oil Crash* (2006), *Deadly Deception: General Electric, Nuclear Weapons and Our Environment* (1991), *Doomwatch* (1972), *An Enemy of the People* (1978), *Erin Brockovich* (2000), *Everything's Cool* (2007), *The Fire Next Time* (1993), *Go Further* (2003), *The Great Global Warming Swindle* (2007), *Green: The New Red, White and Blue* (2007), *I Dreamed of Africa* (2000), *Ice* (1998), *No Blades of Grass* (1970), *Prophecy* (1979), *Quiet Earth* (1985), *Revolution Green* (2007), *Silent Running* (1972), *Soylent Green* (1973), *Sprawling from Grace* (2008), *Taking Back Our Town* (2001), *Texas Gold* (2006), *Toxic Trespass* (2007), *The Waterkeepers* (2000), and *Waterworld* (1995).

A CIVIL ACTION

Genre: Drama

MPAA Rating: PG-13

Alternative Title: None

Directed By: Steven Zaillian

Produced By: Rachel Pfeffer, Robert Redford, and Scott Rudin

Written By: Steven Zaillian

Color: Color

Length: 115 minutes

Language: English

Production Company: Touchstone Pictures

Cast: John Travolta, Robert Duvall, Tony Shalhoub, William H, Macy, John Lithgow, Mary Mara, James Gandolfini, and Dan Hedaya

Film Synopsis

A Civil Action is based on the actual court case of *Anne Anderson v. Cryovac, Inc.* The film is set in Woburn, Massachusetts, and tells the story of an environmental issue that affects the town. Environmental toxins contaminate the town's water supply and as a result a number of local children die. The film focuses on the legal case that is brought against the companies responsible for the toxins. *A Civil Action* was based on the book by the same name written by Jonathan Harr. The film was nominated for two Academy Awards for Best Supporting Actor and Best Cinematography.

AN INCONVENIENT TRUTH

(2006)

Genre: Documentary

MPAA Rating: PG

Alternative Title: None

Directed By: Davis Guggenheim

Produced By: Lawrence Bender, Scott Z. Burns, and Laurie Lennard

Written By: None Credited

Color: Color

Length: 100 minutes

Language: English

Production Company: Lawrence Bender Productions

Cast: Al Gore and Billy West

Film Synopsis

An Inconvenient Truth a documentary that explores the issue of global warming. Former Vice President Al Gore discusses and details the causes and effects global warming has on the world. *An Inconvenient Truth* won two Academy Awards for Best Documentary and Best Original Song.

THE DAY AFTER TOMORROW

(2004)

Genre: Action

MPAA Rating: PG-13

Alternative Title: *Tomorrow*

Directed By: Roland Emmerich

Produced By: Roland Emmerich and Mark Gordon

Written By: Roland Emmerich

Color: Color

Length: 124 minutes

Language: English

Production Company: Twentieth Century-Fox Film Corporation

Cast: Dennis Quaid, Jake Gyllenhaal, Emmy Rossum, Dash Mihok,
Jay O. Sanders, Sela Ward, Austin Nichols, and Ian Holm

Film Synopsis

The Day After Tomorrow depicts the apocalyptic effects of global warming and global cooling. The film tells the story of climatologist Jack Hall (Dennis Quaid), who attempts to save the world from global warming. However, the beginnings of the new ice age unexpectedly comes and Hall must save his son from the frozen tundra that was once New York City. *The Day After Tomorrow* was inspired by the book *The Coming Global Superstorm* by Art Bell and Whitley Strieber.

FUEL

(2008)

Genre: Documentary

MPAA Rating: Not Rated

Alternative Title: *Fields of Fuel*

Directed By: Joshua Tickell

Produced By: Daniel Assael, Darius Fisher, Rebecca Harrell,
and Dale Rosenbloom

Written By: Johnny O'Hara

Color: Color

Length: 112 minutes

Language: English

Production Company: Blue Water Entertainment

Cast: Barbara Boxer, Richard Branson, George W. Bush, Sheryl Crow,
Jimmy Carter, Woody Harrelson, Ronald Reagan, Deborah Dupre,
and Larry David

Film Synopsis

Fuel is a documentary that explores and examines the demand for energy. The film examines the connections between the government, oil companies, and automobile manufacturers. The film also discusses the use of alternative energies such as solar, wind, and biofuels. In addition, the film chronicles America's addiction to oil and its connection to the economy.

THE GREEN CHAIN

(2007)

Genre: Drama

MPAA Rating: Not Rated

Alternative Title: None

Directed By: Mark Leiren-Young

Produced By: Mark Leiren-Young and Tony Wosk

Written By: Mark Leiren-Young

Color: Color

Length: 90 minutes

Language: English

Production Company: I Love Trees Productions Inc.

Cast: Tricia Helfer, Brenden Fletcher, Tahmoh Penikett, Babs Chula, Jillian Fargey, Scott McNeil, and August Schellenberg

Film Synopsis

The Green Chain portrays the confrontation between loggers and environmentalists. The film tells the story of a community and the varying perspectives held by its populous. It highlights the conflict between loggers and those opposed to the destruction of forest land.

WHO KILLED THE ELECTRIC CAR?

(2006)

Genre: Documentary

MPAA Rating: PG

Alternative Title: None

Directed By: Chris Paine

Produced By: Jessie Deeter

Written By: Chris Paine

Color: Color

Length: 92 minutes

Language: English

Production Company: Plinyminor

Cast: Martin Sheen, Reverend Gadget, Dave Barthmuss, Ed Begley Jr., Jim Boyd, Alec N. Brooks, Colette Divine, and Mel Gibson

Film Synopsis

Who Killed the Electric Car? is a film that chronicles the creation, limited distribution, and destruction of the electric car. The film examines the causes for the destruction of electric cars, specifically General Motors EV1, and the connection between automobile manufacturers, oil companies, and the government. The film also discusses the role of renewable energy in society.

Gang Culture

Gang culture has been depicted on film in various ways. Gang culture as a topic has come and gone as gang culture reasserts itself into the national spotlight. Gang culture is simply the activities and lifestyle of gangs and their members. Many films depict specific illegal activities, which can include the sale of drugs and/or stolen goods and various types of violence gangs can partake in. Gang culture became a more significant topic in films during the last 30–40 years, focusing on racial and ethnic urban gangs, like the Bloods and the Crips. Films relevant to gang culture can often pertain to other social issues such as hate groups and racism. However, these social issues are handled separately in this chapter.

Other films dealing with gang culture not detailed in this volume include: *15: The Movie* (2003), *American History X* (1998), *Bad Boy* (2004), *Beantown* (2007), *Boyz N the Hood* (1991), *Brother* (2000), *Corrupt* (1999), *City Across the River* (1949), *Cry-Baby* (1990), *Dangerous Minds* (1995), *Deuces Wild* (2002), *Gangs of New York* (2002), *Gran Torino* (2008), *Hells Angels on Wheels* (1967), *Juice* (1992), *Key Witness* (1960), *Mad at the World* (1955), *A Man Apart* (2003), *My Crazy Life* (1993), *On the Downlow* (2004), *The Red Skulls* (2005), *Redemption: The Stan Tookie Williams Story* (2004), *Rumble Fish* (1983), *Slippin': Ten Years with the Bloods* (2005), *South Central* (1992), *The Wanderers* (1979), *The Warriors* (1979), *Why We Bang* (2006), and *The Wild One* (1953).

AMERICAN ME

(1992)

Genre: Biography

MPAA Rating: R

Alternative Title: None

Directed By: Edward James Olmos

Produced By: Sean Daniel, Edward James Olmos, and Robert M. Young

Written By: Floyd Mutrux

Color: Color

Length: 125 minutes

Language: English

Production Company: Universal Pictures

Cast: Edward James Olmos, Sal Lopez, Vira Montes, Roberto Martín Márquez, Dyana Ortelli, William Forsythe, and Richard Coca

Film Synopsis

American Me was inspired by the true story of the founder of the Mexican mafia, Rodolfo Cadena. The film tells the story of Santana (Edward James Olmos), a Mexican American who spends a great deal of his life in prison. While serving an 18- year sentence, Santana establishes the Mexican mafia and quickly rises to power, which spreads outside of the prison walls.

BLOOD IN, BLOOD OUT

(1993)

Genre: Action

MPAA Rating: R

Alternative Title: *Bound by Honor*

Directed By: Taylor Hackford

Produced By: Jerry Gershwin and Taylor Hackford

Written By: Jimmy Santiago Baca

Color: Color

Length: 180 minutes

Language: English

Production Company: Hollywood Pictures

Cast: Damian Chapa, Jesse Borrego, Delroy Lindo, Victor Rivers, Billy Bob Thornton, Teddy Wilson, Raymond Cruz, and Valente Rodriguez

Film Synopsis

Blood In, Blood Out is based on the real-life experiences of Jimmy Santiago Baca, a Mexican American writer and poet. The film chronicles the lives of three relatives during the 1970s and 1980s. The film specifically focuses on their membership in the East Los Angeles gang known as the "Vatos Locos" and the separates paths that gang life leads them.

BRA BOYS: BLOOD IS THICKER THAN WATER

(2007)

Genre: Documentary

MPAA Rating: R

Alternative Title: None

Directed By: Sunny Abberton and Macario De Souza

Produced By: Sunny Abberton

Written By: Sunny Abberton and Stuart Beattie

Color: Color

Length: 90 minutes

Language: English

Production Company: Bradahood Productions

Cast: Russell Crowe, Kelly Slater, Cheyne Horan, Jack Kingsley, Sean Doherty, Koby Abberton, John Gannon, and Maurice Cole

Film Synopsis

Bra Boys: Blood is Thicker than Water is a documentary film that examines and explores the notorious Australian surf gang known as the Bra Boys. The film highlights the origins of the gang, their continuous clashes with authorities, and their social deviances in Maroubra, a suburb of Sydney.

COLORS

(1988)

Genre: Crime

MPAA Rating: R

Alternative Title: None

Directed By: Dennis Hopper

Produced By: Robert H. Solo

Written By: Michael Schiffer

Color: Color

Length: 120 minutes

Language: English

Production Company: Orion Pictures Corporation

Cast: Sean Penn, Robert Duvall, Maria Conchita Alonso,
Randy Brooks, Grand L. Bush, Don Cheadle, Glenn Plummer,
Gerardo Mejía, and Damon Wayans

Film Synopsis

Colors is set in South Central Los Angeles and tells the story of two police officers who attempt to eliminate local gang violence. The film focuses on Bob Hodges (Robert Duvall), a veteran police officer, and his rookie partner, Danny McGavin (Sean Penn), and how they attempt to maintain order and justice among the violent clashes between the Bloods and the Crips.

THE OUTSIDERS

(1983)

Genre: Crime

MPAA Rating: PG-13

Alternative Title: None

Directed By: Francis Ford Coppola

Produced By: Gray Frederickson and Fred Roos

Written By: Kathleen Rowell

Color: Color

Length: 91 minutes

Language: English

Production Company: Zoetrope Studios

Cast: C. Thomas Howell, Matt Dillon, Emilio Estevez, Tom Cruise,
Patrick Swayze, Rob Lowe, Ralph Macchio, and Darren Dalton

Film Synopsis

The Outsiders portrays two rival gangs and the violence that is caused by their hatred. The film tells the story of the Greasers and the Socs, who continuously battle for turf and power. *The Outsiders* is based on the book by the same name written by S.E. Hinton.

WEST SIDE STORY

(1961)

Genre: Musical

MPAA Rating: R

Alternative Title: None

Directed By: Jerome Robbins and Robert Wise

Produced By: Robert Wise

Written By: Ernest Lehman

Color: Color

Length: 152 minutes

Language: English

Production Company: The Mirisch Corporation

Cast: Natalie Wood, Richard Beymer, Russ Tamblyn, Rita Moreno, George Chakiris, Simon Oakland, Ned Glass, and David Bean

Film Synopsis

West Side Story is a musical about two lovers, each from a rival gang in New York City. The film tells the story of Tony (Richard Beymer), a white Jet, and Maria (Natalie Wood), a Puerto Rican Shark, and their forbidden relationship. Tony and Maria's secret love provokes a battle between the rival gangs for control of the streets. *West Side Story* was adapted for the screen from William Shakespeare's *Romeo and Juliet*. The film won 10 Academy Awards, including Best Picture, Best Director, and Best Cinematography.

Genocide

> *There is a flaw in human nature that, if allowed full rein, leads to suspicion, alienation, victimization, and finally even genocide—the "final solution."*
>
> —Desmond M. Tutu

Genocide can be defined as "any of the following acts committed with intent to destroy, in whole or in part, a national, ethnical, racial or religious group, as such: (a) Killing members of the group; (b) Causing serious bodily or mental harm to members of the group; (c) Deliberately inflicting on the group conditions of life calculated to bring about its physical destruction in whole or in part; (d) Imposing measures intended to prevent births within the group; (e) Forcibly transferring children of the group to another group" (United Nations, 1948, Article 2). Genocide-related events have often been depicted in films. The large majority of films pertaining to genocide portray the atrocities of the Holocaust. However, there have been and/or currently are other genocides that need to be examined, such as Armenian genocide, the atrocities in Rwanda, and genocide in Darfur.

Other films dealing with genocide not detailed in this volume include: *Armenian Genocide* (2006), *Blood Diamond* (2006), *Darfur Diaries* (2006), *Death of a Nation: The Timor Conspiracy* (1994), *The Devil Came on Horseback* (2007), *Facing Sudan* (2007), *Final Solution* (2003), *Genocide* (1982), *The Grey Zone* (2001), *Harrison's Flower* (2004), *Katyn* (2007), *Kundun* (1997), *The Last King of Scotland* (2006), *Life is Beautiful* (1997), *Night and Fog* (1955), *Paragraph 175* (2000), *The Pianist* (2002), *Screamers* (2006), *Shake Hands With The Devil* (2007), *Shake Hands with the Devil: The Journey of Romeo Dallaire* (2004), *Sometimes In April* (2005), *Tears of the Sun* (2003), *The Translator* (2009), *Warriors* (1999), and *Welcome to Sarajevo* (1997).

ARARAT

(2002)

Genre: Drama

MPAA Rating: R

Alternative Title: None

Directed By: Atom Egoyan

Produced By: Atom Egoyan and Robert Lantos

Written By: Atom Egoyan

Color: Color

Length: 115 minutes

Language: English

Production Company: Alliance Atlantis Communications

Cast: Simon Abkarian, Christopher Plummer, Charles Aznavour, David Alplay, Arsinée Khanjian, Elias Koteas, Setta Keshishian, and Brent Carver

Film Synopsis

Ararat depicts the Armenian genocide during World War I, through a film within a film. The storyline depicts the story of a man and how his life was transformed during his employment on the film set of a movie about the Armenian genocide.

DARFUR NOW

(2007)

Genre: Documentary

MPAA Rating: PG

Alternative Title: None

Directed By: Ted Braun

Produced By: Don Cheadle, Mark Jonathan Harris, and Cathy Schulman

Written By: Ted Braun

Color: Color

Length: 98 minutes

Language: English

Production Company: Crescendo Productions

Cast: Ahmed Mahammed Abaka, Sheikh Ahmed Mohamad Abakar, Hawa Abaker, Hejewa Adam, Don Cheadle, George Clooney, Hillary Clinton, and John McCain

Film Synopsis

Darfur Now is a documentary that explores the genocide currently taking place in Sudan's western region of Darfur. The film portrays six different individuals' responses to the atrocities in Darfur. The film examines the genocide in Darfur through the experiences of (1) Adam Sterling, a 24-year-old waiter and activist; (2) Don Cheadle, an Academy Award–nominated actor; (3) Luis Moreno-Ocampo, a prosecutor of the International Criminal Court in The Hague, Netherlands; (4) Hejewa Adam, a woman in Darfur whose baby was beaten to death by Janjaweed attackers; (5) Ahmed Mohammed Abakar, a leader of a camp for displaced Darfurians; and (6) Pablo Recalde, the leader of the World Food Program in West Darfur.

HOTEL RWANDA

(2004)

Genre: Drama

MPAA Rating: PG-13

Alternative Title: None

Directed By: Terry George

Produced By: Terry George and A. Kitman Ho

Written By: Keir Pearson and Terry Geogre

Color: Color

Length: 121 Minutes

Language: English

Production Company: United Artists

Cast: Don Cheadle, Nick Nolte, Joaquin Phoenix, Sophie Okonedo, and Hakeem Kae-Kazim

Film Synopsis

Hotel Rwanda is set in 1994, during the Rwandan genocide in which an estimated 1 million Tutsi were murdered by Hutu militias. This movie tells the true story of Paul Rusesabagina (Don Cheadle), a hotel manager who provided shelter to over a thousand Tutsi refugees during the besiegement by the Hutu militias. *Hotel Rwanda* was nominated for three Academy Awards, including Best Actor and Best Original Screenplay.

THE KILLING FIELDS

Genre: Drama

MPAA Rating: R

Alternative Title: None

Directed By: Roland Joffé

Produced By: David Puttnam

Written By: Bruce Robinson

Color: Color

Length: 140 minutes

Language: English

Production Company: Enigma

Cast: Sam Waterson, Haing S. Ngor, John Malkovich, Julian Sands, Craig T. Nelson, Spalding Gray, Athol Fugard, and Bill Paterson

Film Synopsis

The Killing Fields is based on the true story of three journalists trapped in Cambodia during the Cambodian genocide where approximately 1.7 million Cambodians were killed. *The Killing Fields* was inspired by Sydney Schanberg's book, *The Death and Life of Dith Pran*. The film was nominated for seven Academy Awards in which it won three, including Best Actor in a Supporting Role (Haing S. Ngor) and Best Cinematography.

SCHINDLER'S LIST

(1993)

Genre: Drama

MPAA Rating: R

Alternative Title: N/A

Directed By: Steven Spielberg

Produced By: Branko Lustig, Gerald Molen, and Steven Spielberg

Written By: Steven Zaillian

Color: Black and white/Color

Length: 195 Minutes

Language: English

Production Company: Universal Pictures

Cast: Liam Neeson, Ben Kingsley, Ralph Fiennes, Caroline Goodall, Jonathan Sagall, Embeth Davidtz, and Mark Ivanir

Film Synopsis

Schindler's List is based on the true story of Oskar Schindler (Liam Neeson), a businessman and a member of the Nazi Party, who helped save the lives of over 1,000 Jews during the Holocaust by having them work in his factories. *Schindler's List* is based on Thomas Keneally's 1982 Booker Prize–winning book, *Schindler's Ark*. The film won seven Academy Awards, including Best Picture and Best Director.

SHOOTING DOGS

(2005)

Genre: Drama

MPAA Rating: R

Alternative Title: *Beyond the Gates*

Directed By: Michael Caton-Jones

Produced By: David Belton, Pippa Cross, and Jens Meurer

Written By: David Wolstencroft

Color: Color

Length: 115 minutes

Language: English

Production Company: CrossDay Productions Ltd.

Cast: John Hurt, Hugh Dancy, Dominique Horwitz, Louis Mahoney, Nicola Walker, Steve Toussaint, David Gyasi, and Victor Power

Film Synopsis

Shooting Dogs is set in 1994 during the Rwandan genocide, in the Ecole Technique Officielle in Kigali, Rwanda. The film tells the story of a Catholic priest (John Hurt) and an English teacher (Hugh Dancy) who provide shelter to over 1,000 Tutsi refugees.

Gun Control

Gun control is one social issue that has not received the specific attention many consider it needs. Gun control as a social issue pertains to the legal and constitutional rights of citizens to own, use, and regulate a firearm. Guns are often a regular figure in movies. The overt depiction of gun use in films is a powerful statement in itself. Films relevant to gun control can often pertain to other social issues such as role of government. However, this social issue is handled separately in this chapter.

Other films dealing with gun control not detailed in this volume include: *Bowling for Columbine* (2002), *Bullets in the Hood: A Bed-Stuy Story* (2005), *Innocents Betrayed* (2003), *Liberty Stands Still* (2002), *Waco: The Rules of Engagement* (1997), *Walking with Guns* (2008), and *Wasted! Guns and Teens, Lives and Dreams* (2004).

AMERICAN GUN

(2005)

Genre: Drama

MPAA Rating: R

Alternative Title: None

Directed By: Aric Avelino

Produced By: Ted Kroeber

Written By: Aric Avelino and Steven Bagatourian

Color: Color

Length: 95 minutes

Language: English

Production Company: IFC Films

Cast: Marcia Gay Harden, Forest Whitaker, Donald Sutherland, Lisa Long, Chris Warren Jr., David Heymann, Chris Marquette, and Rex Linn

Film Synopsis

American Gun portrays the impact guns have on individuals of all backgrounds. The film tells three different stories focusing on the proliferation of firearms in America. The characters include a principal of an inner-city school, a single mother, and college student who works at her grandfather's gun shop.

GUNS AND MOTHERS

(2003)

Genre: Documentary

MPAA Rating: Not Rated

Alternative Title: None

Directed By: Thom Powers

Produced By: Thom Powers, Meema Spadola, and John W. Walter

Written By: None Credited

Color: Color

Length: 55 minutes

Language: English

Production Company: Sugar Pictures

Cast: Maria Heil and Frances Davis

Film Synopsis

Guns & Mothers is a documentary that examines the issue of gun control. The film explores the continuous debate over gun control through the viewpoints of two mothers on opposite sides of the spectrum. Maria Heil is a spokeswoman for the Second Amendment Sisters and a mother of four. Frances Davis is an advocate of gun control and a mother of three deceased sons, all victims of gun violence.

LORD OF WAR

(2005)

Genre: Crime

MPAA Rating: R

Alternative Title: None

Directed By: Andrew Niccol

Produced By: Nicholas Cage, Norman Golightly, Andrew Niccol, Philippe Rousselet, and Chris Roberts

Written By: Andrew Niccol

Color: Color

Length: 122 minutes

Language: English

Production Company: Entertainment Manufacturing Company

Cast: Nicholas Cage, Bridget Moynahan, Jared Leto, Shake Tukhmanyan, Jared Burke, David Shumbris, Eric Uys, Stewart Morgan, and Ethan Hawke

Film Synopsis

Lord of War is based on actual events and portrays the life of an illegal arms dealer. The film chronicles the life of Yuri Orlov (Nicholas Cage), from his origins as a small-time gun dealer in the 1980s to his rise in power in the 1990s. Yuri becomes a central figure in the illegal arms trade and sin-gle-handedly arms African warlords and their armies. The film highlights the trafficking of guns and the role firearms play in violent conflicts around the world.

MICHAEL AND ME

(2004)

Genre: Documentary

MPAA Rating: Not Rated

Alternative Title: None

Directed By: Larry Elder

Produced By: Larry Elder

Written By: Larry Elder

Color: Color

Length: 90 minutes

Language: English

Production Company: Maiden Voyage Productions Inc.

Cast: Larry Elder and Michael Moore

Film Synopsis

Michael & Me is a documentary that attempts to disprove some of the conclusions made by Michael Moore in his film, *Bowling for Columbine*. The film examines and attempts to disprove the connection between American culture, gun ownership, and increased gun violence.

THE RIGHT OF THE PEOPLE

(1986)

Genre: Drama

MPAA Rating: Not Rated

Alternative Title: None

Directed By: Jeffrey Bloom

Produced By: Thomas Fries

Written By: None Credited

Color: Color

Length: 100 minutes

Language: English

Production Company: Big Name Films

Cast: Michael Ontkean, Billy Dee Williams, John Randolph, Jane Kaczmarek, Jamie Smith-Jackson, M. Emmet Walsh, Jeffrey Josephson, and Janet Carroll

Film Synopsis

The Right of the People tells the story of a small town that votes to allow its residents to protect themselves by carrying firearms. After a tragic and brutal shooting, the father of the slain child persuades the city council to approve legislation that allows residents to carry firearms.

RUNAWAY JURY

(2003)

Genre: Drama

MPAA Rating: PG-13

Alternative Title: None

Directed By: Gary Fleder

Produced By: Gary Fleder, Christopher Mankiewicz, and Arnon Milchan

Written By: Brian Koppelman

Color: Color

Length: 127 minutes

Language: English

Production Company: Regency Enterprises

Cast: John Cusack, Gene Hackman, Dustin Hoffman, Rachel Weisz, Jeremy Piven, Bruce Davison, Bruce McGill, Nick Searcy, and Cliff Curtis

Film Synopsis

Runaway Jury depicts the events surrounding the trial against a major gun manufacturer. A widow whose husband was killed at work by a disgruntled employee files a lawsuit against the gun manufacturer. The film focuses on Nicholas (John Cusack), a jury member, and his attempts to manipulate the outcome of the trial. *Runaway Jury* was adapted for the screen from John Grisham's novel, *The Runaway Jury*.

Hate Groups

Hate groups are simply groups of individuals who believe and promote hate of others. Hate groups have been depicted in movies since the birth of cinema. No depiction of a hate group is probably more infamous than that of the Ku Klux Klan (KKK) in *Birth of a Nation* (1915). The KKK, white nationalists, neo-Nazis, and skinheads have all been well documented on film. Hate groups like The Nation of Islam and anti-gay groups have been depicted sparingly in films. Other hate groups, such as the New Black Panther

Party, the Jewish Defense League, Holocaust deniers, and black separatists, have not received significant attention from Hollywood. Many films depict hate groups or actions of hate groups. Films relevant to hate groups can pertain to other social issues, such as racism, gang violence, and terrorism. However, these social issues are handled separately in this chapter.

Other films dealing with hate groups not detailed in this volume include: *Ali* (2001), *American History X* (1998), *Anatomy of a Hate Crime* (2001), *Attack on Terror: The FBI vs. The Ku Klux Klan* (1975), *Black Legion* (1936), *Blood in the Face* (1991), *The Burning Cross* (1947), *The California Reich* (1975), *Confessions of a Nazi Spy* (1939), *Cross of Fire* (1989), *Death of a Prophet* (1981), *The Hate That Hate Produced* (1959), *Higher Learning* (1995), *The Intruder* (1962), *The Klansman* (1974), *The Legion of Terror* (1937), *Louis and the Nazis* (2003), *Made in Britain* (1982), *Malcolm X* (1992), *Nazi America: A Secret History* (2000), *No Way Out* (1950), *O Brother, Where Art Thou?* (2000), *Oi! Warning* (1999), *Pressure Point* (1962), *Roots: The Next Generation* (1979), *Skinhead Attitude* (2003), *Skinheads* (1989), *So Proudly We Hail* (1990), *Storm Warning* (1950), *Strange Holiday* (1942), *They Came to Blow Up America* (1943), *This is England* (2006), and *Trial* (1955).

THE BELIEVER

(2001)

Genre: Drama

MPAA Rating: R

Alternative Title: None

Directed By: Henry Bean

Produced By: Christopher Roberts and Susan Hoffman

Written By: Henry Bean

Color: Color

Length: 102 minutes

Language: English

Production Company: Fuller Films

Cast: Ryan Gosling, Peter Meadows, Garret Dillahunt, Billy Zane, Joel Garland, Theresa Russell, Kris Eivers, and Ronald Guttman

Film Synopsis

The Believer is based on the true story of Dan Burros, who was a member of the American Nazi Party and the Ku Klux Klan, despite being Jewish. The film tells the story of Danny Balint (Ryan Gosling), who is a self-hating Jewish man that becomes a violent anti-Semitic neo-Nazi. The film chronicles Danny's rise through the ranks of the neo-Nazi Party and his mental struggles with his cultural and religious heritage. *The Believer* won the Grand Jury Prize at the Sundance Film Festival.

BETRAYED

(1988)

Genre: Drama

MPAA Rating: R

Alternative Title: *Summer Lightning*

Directed By: Costa-Gavras

Produced By: Irwin Winkler

Written By: Joe Eszterhas

Color: Color

Length: 127 minutes

Language: English

Production Company: CST Telecommunications

Cast: Debra Winger, Tom Berenger, John Heard, Betsy Blair, John Mahoney, Ted Levine, Albert Hall, Brian Bosak, and Alan Wilder

Film Synopsis

Betrayed tells the story of an undercover FBI agent, Catherine Weaver (Debra Winger), who is searching for the hate group responsible for the murder of a Jewish radio host. While on assignment, she falls in love with a local man, Gary Simmons (Tom Berenger), who turns out to be the leader of the hate group.

THE BIRTH OF A NATION

(1915)

Genre: Drama

MPAA Rating: Not Rated

Alternative Title: *The Clansman*

Directed By: D. W. Griffith

Produced By: D.W. Griffith

Written By: Thomas F. Dixon Jr.

Color: Black and white

Length: 187 minutes

Language: English

Production Company: David W. Griffith Corp.

Cast: Lillian Gish, Mae Marsh, Henry B. Walthall, Miriam Cooper,
Mary Alden, Ralph Lewis, George Siegmann, Joseph Henabery,
and Walter Long

Film Synopsis

The Birth of a Nation is set during the Civil War era and tells the story of two families on opposite sides of the war. The film portrays the effects the war has on life and depicts the creation of the Ku Klux Klan and the hate crimes that follow. The film is based on the book *The Clansman*, by Thomas Dixon.

FOCUS

(2002)

Genre: Drama

MPAA Rating: PG-13

Alternative Title: None

Directed By: Neil Slavin

Produced By: Robert A. Miller and Neil Slavin

Written By: Kendrew Lascelles

Color: Color

Length: 106 minutes

Language: English

Production Company: Carros Pictures

Cast: William H. Macy, Laura Dern, Meat Loaf, David Paymer,
Key Hawtrey, Michael Copeman, Kenneth Welsh,
and Peter Oldring

Film Synopsis

Focus is set in Brooklyn, New York, after World War II and tells the story of a married couple, Larry and Gert (William H. Macy and Laura Dern), who are mistakenly thought to be Jewish by anti-Semitic neighbors. The film portrays the religious and racial prejudice the couple faces and how they deal with the hatred, violence, and discrimination. *Focus* is based on Arthur Miller's novel by the same name.

ROMPER STOMPER

(1992)

Genre: Action

MPAA Rating: R

Alternative Title: None

Directed By: Geoffrey Wright

Produced By: Daniel Scharf and Ian Pringle

Written By: Geoffrey Wright

Color: Color

Length: 94 minutes

Language: English

Production Company: The Australian Film Commission

Cast: Russell Crowe, Daniel Pollock, Jacqueline McKenzie, Alex Scott, Leigh Russell, Daniel Wyllie, James McKenna, Eric Mueck, and Frank Magree

Film Synopsis

Romper Stomper tells the story of a group of neo-Nazi skinheads in Melbourne, Australia. The film depicts the feelings and actions the skinheads take against Vietnamese immigrants, who they consider to be a threat to racial purity in Melbourne.

STEEL TOES

(2006)

Genre: Drama

MPAA Rating: R

Alternative Title: None

Directed By: Mark Adam and David Gow

Produced By: Francine Allaire and David Gow

Written By: David Gow

Color: Color

Length: 90 minutes

Language: English

Production Company: Monterey Media

Cast: David Strathairn, Andrew W. Walker, Marina Orsini, Ivana Shein, Linda Smith, Aaron Grunfeld, Joel Miller, and Ron Lea

Film Synopsis

Steel Toes tells the story of Danny Dunckelman (David Strathairn), a Jewish defense lawyer who is assigned to defend Mike Downey (Andrew Walker), a neo-Nazi skinhead charged for a racially motivated murder. The film examines their relationship and the differing beliefs that each hold.

Homosexuality

Homosexuality is a very relevant and popular issue in today's society. Throughout the history of film, homosexuals have been portrayed in numerous ways through various characters. However, it was not until more recently that homosexuals and their rights became a central theme of movies. Films pertaining to homosexuality discussed in this volume deal with the life of homosexuals and their rights as citizens. Films relevant to homosexuality can often pertain to other social issues such as AIDS, hate groups, and religion. However, these social issues are handled separately in this chapter.

Other films dealing with homosexuality not detailed in this volume include: *After Stonewall* (1999), *And the Band Played On* (1993), *Before Stonewall* (1984), *The Birdcage* (1996), *Boys Don't Cry* (1999), *The Boys in the Band* (1970), *Brokeback Mountain* (2005), *Brother Outsider: The Life of Bayard Rustin* (2003), *Cruising* (1980), *A Different Story* (1978), *The Education of Shelby Knox* (2005), *Flawless* (1999), *For Love and for Life: The 1987 March on Washington for Lesbian and Gay Rights* (1990), *A Jihad for Love* (2007), *The Laramie Project* (2002), *Maple Palm* (2006), *The Naked Civil Servant* (1975), *One Summer in New Paltz: A Cautionary Tale* (2008), *Philadelphia* (1993), *Prom Queen: The Marc Hall Story* (2004), *Politics of the Heart* (2005), *Pursuit of Equality* (2005), *Same Sex America* (2006), *The Times of Harvey Milk* (1984), *Traveling to Olympia* (2001), *Wedding Wars* (2006), and *Welcome Home Bobby* (1986).

EXECUTION OF JUSTICE

(1999)

Genre: Crime

MPAA Rating: R

Alternative Title: None

Directed By: Leon Ichaso

Produced By: Jeff Freilich

Written By: Michael Butler

Color: Color

Length: 98 minutes

Language: English

Production Company: Daly-Harris Productions

Cast: Tim Daly, Peter Coyote, Khalil Kain, Stephen Young, Tyne Daly, Lisa Rhoden, Frank Pellegrino, Amy Van Nostrand, and Mark Camacho

Film Synopsis

Execution of Justice is a made-for-television film based on the true story of the assassination of the openly gay San Francisco Mayor, George Moscone, and City Supervisor, Harvey Milk. The film chronicles the trial of Dan White (Tim Daly) for the murder of George Moscone (Stephen Young) and Harvey Milk (Peter Coyote), including the notorious "Twinkie defense" strategy used by White's lawyers. *Execution of Justice* is based on the play by the same name written by Emily Mann.

KINSEY

(2004)

Genre: Biography

MPAA Rating: R

Alternative Title: None

Directed By: Bill Condon

Produced By: Gail Mutrux

Written By: Bill Condon

Color: Color

Length: 118 minutes

Language: English

Production Company: Fox Searchlight Pictures

Cast: Liam Neeson, Laura Linney, Chris O'Donnell, Peter Sarsgaard, John Lithgow, Timothy Hutton, Oliver Platt, and William Sadler

Film Synopsis

Kinsey is a biographical film that depicts the life of Alfred Kinsey, who was a well-known scientist and is considered the father of sexology. The film portrays Alfred Kinsey's (Liam Neeson) life and details the events and research he conducted about human sexuality. The film highlights Kinsey's marriage and other physical relationships he had with both men and women. *Kinsey* was nominated for an Academy Award for Best Supporting Actress (Laura Linney) and was also nominated for three Golden Globes, including Best Motion Picture.

MILK

(2008)

Genre: Biography

MPAA Rating: R

Alternative Title: *Untitled Harvey Milk Project*

Directed By: Gus Van Sant

Produced By: Bruce Cohen, Dan Jenks, and Michael London

Written By: Dustin Lance Black

Color: Color

Length: 128 minutes

Language: English

Production Company: Focus Features

Cast: Sean Penn, Emile Hirsch, Josh Brolin, Diego Luna, James Franco, Alison Pill, Joseph Cross, Victor Garber, and Brandon Boyce

Film Synopsis

Milk is a biographical film that recounts the life of Harvey Milk, the first openly gay politician to be elected to a major public office in California. The film chronicles Harvey Milk's (Sean Penn) political career and his relationship with Dan White (Josh Brolin), a conservative politician who eventually murders Harvey Milk and San Francisco Mayor George Moscone (Victor Garber). *Milk* was nominated for eight Academy Awards, in which it won Best Screenplay and Best Actor (Sean Penn).

SERVING IN SILENCE: THE MARGARETHE CAMMERMEYER STORY

(1995)

Genre: Biography

MPAA Rating: Not Rated

Alternative Title: *Serving in Silence: The Colonel Grethe Cammermeyer Story*

Directed By: Jeff Bleckner

Produced By: Richard Heus

Written By: Alison Cross

Color: Color

Length: 91 minutes

Language: English

Production Company: Barwood Films

Cast: Glenn Close, Judy Davis, Jan Rubes, Wendy Makkena, Susan Barnes, William Allen Young, Eric Dane, Ryan Reynolds, and Molly Parker

Film Synopsis

Serving in Silence: The Margarethe Cammermeyer Story is a made-for-television film based on the true story of Colonel Margarethe Cammermeyer (Glenn Close), focusing on her discharge from the Washington National Guard for being a lesbian and her battle for her rights. The film was nominated for six Emmy Awards, of which it won three—Outstanding Writing, Outstanding Actress (Glenn Close), and Outstanding Supporting Actress (Judy Davis).

STONEWALL

(1995)

Genre: Drama

MPAA Rating: R

Alternative Title: None

Directed By: Nigel Finch

Produced By: Christine Vachon and Ruth Caleb

Written By: Rikki Beadle Blair

Color: Color

Length: 99 minutes

Language: English

Production Company: British Broadcasting Corporation

Cast: Guillermo Díaz, Fred Weller, Brendan Corbalis, Duane Boutte,
Bruce MacVittie, Dwight Ewell, Peter Ratray, and Joey Dedio

Film Synopsis

Stonewall is based on true events surrounding the Stonewall riots, which is considered the defining event that started the modern-day gay rights movement in the United States. The film tells a fictional story that recounts the weeks leading up to the Stonewall riots and highlights the causes of the monumental event that started on June 28, 1969, in Greenwich Village at the Stonewall Inn.

TYING THE KNOT

(2004)

Genre: Documentary

MPAA Rating: Not Rated

Alternative Title: None

Directed By: Jim de Sève

Produced By: Kian T. Jong, Jim de Sève, and Stephen Pelletier

Written By: None credited

Color: Color

Length: 81 minutes

Language: English

Production Company: 1,049 Films

Cast: Bob Barr, Mary Bonauto, Brian Brown, Martin Bubbly,
Rev. Pat Bumgardner, Charles Cannady, Jane E. Castor,
Francis Ford Coppola, and Larry King

Film Synopsis

Tying the Knot is a documentary that examines and explores same-sex marriage in the United States. The film analyzes the issue from both sides and includes interviews and discussions with same-sex couples and those opposed to same-sex marriage.

Immigration

Immigration is simply the migration of an individual from one country to another country. Immigration is a social issue that receives a great deal of attention, especially around the election of public officials. Immigration, as a central theme of movies, has recently received much more attention. Films relevant to immigration can often pertain to other social issues such as consumerism, labor practices, and role of government. However, these social issues are handled separately in this chapter.

Other films dealing with immigration not detailed in this volume include: *Across the Sea of Time* (1995), *The Betrayel—Nerakhoon* (2008), *Border Incident* (1949), *Casa Libre/Freedom House* (2008), *Come Live with Me* (1941), *Crossing Arizona* (2006), *Dancer in the Dark* (2000), *Dondi* (1961), *Dying to Get In: Undocumented Immigration at the U.S. Mexican Border* (2005), *Ellis Island* (1984), *Far and Away* (1992), *Farmingville* (2004), *Fast Food Nation* (2006), *Flower Drum Song* (1961), *Gangs of New York* (2002), *The Girl Who Spelled Freedom* (1986), *The Glass Wall* (1953), *The Godfather: Part II* (1974), *Gran Torino* (2008), *Green Card* (1990), *Heaven's Gate* (1980), *Hold Back the Dawn* (1941), *The Kite Runner* (2007), *Joe Hill* (1971), *Lonely in America* (1991), *Lost in Gainesville* (2006), *Made in L.A.* (2007), *Maple Palm* (2006), *The Mortal Storm* (1940), *Moscow on the Hudson* (1984), *Now Chinatown* (2000), *On the Line* (1984), *Out of Ireland* (1995), *The Perez Family* (1990), *The Return of Rusty* (1946), *Romance in Manhattan* (1935), *Salt of the Earth* (1954), *Scarface* (1983), *The Second Civil War* (1997), *The Terminal* (2004), and *Walking the Line* (2005).

A DAY WITHOUT A MEXICAN

(2004)

Genre: Comedy

MPAA Rating: R

Alternative Title: None

Directed By: Sergio Arau

Produced By: Isaac Artenstein

Written By: Yareli Arizmendi and Sergio Arau

Color: Color

Length: 100 minutes

Language: English

Production Company: Eye On the Ball Films

Cast: Caroline Aaron, Tony Abatemarco, Melinda Allen, Frankie J. Allison, Yareli Arizmendi, Todd Babcock, Yareli Arizmendi, and Maria Beck

Film Synopsis

A Day without a Mexican is a satirical portrayal of life in California without Latinos. The film focuses on the stories of three individuals, a wife who searches for her husband, a Senator who loses his housekeeper, and a farmer who loses his migrant workers. The film details the sudden disappearance of Latinos and the impact it has on the state and its economy.

AN AMERICAN TAIL

(1986)

Genre: Animation

MPAA Rating: G

Alternative Title: None

Directed By: Don Bluth

Produced By: Don Bluth, Gary Goldman, and John Pomeroy

Written By: Judy Freudberg

Color: Color

Length: 80 minutes

Language: English

Production Company: Amblin Entertainment

Cast: Erica Yohn, Nehemiah Persoff, Amy Green, Phillip Glasser, Christopher Plummer, John Finnegan, Will Ryan, Madeline Kahn, and Dom DeLuise

Film Synopsis

An American Tail is an animated film about a Russian family of mice immigrating to the United States. The film tells the story of a young mouse named Fievel, who gets separated from his family during the move. Fievel embarks on a wondrous journey in search for his family and attempts to survey the hardships and dangers of his new country. *An American Tail* won a Grammy Award for Best Original Song for "Somewhere Out There."

BORDER WAR: THE BATTLE OVER ILLEGAL IMMIGRATION

(2006)

Genre: Documentary

MPAA Rating: Not Rated

Alternative Title: None

Directed By: Kevin Knoblock

Produced By: Christopher T. Bannon, David Bossie, and Stephen K. Bannon

Written By: Kevin Knoblock

Color: Color

Length: 95 minutes

Language: English

Production Company: Genius Products

Cast: J.D. Hayworth, Lupe Moreno, Enrique Morones, Teri March, and Jose Maheda

Film Synopsis

Border War: The Battle Over Illegal Immigration is a documentary that examines and explores illegal immigration along the United States–Mexico border. The film focuses on five individuals that have been directly impacted by illegal immigration. The individuals highlighted are a widow whose husband was killed by an illegal immigrant, a Congressman in Arizona, a United States Border Patrol agent, and two illegal immigrant sympathizers. The film takes viewers into the smuggling tunnels and halfway houses along the U.S.–Mexico border.

IN AMERICA

(2002)

Genre: Drama

MPAA Rating: PG-13

Alternative Title: *East of Harlem*

Directed By: Jim Sheridan

Produced By: Arthur Lappin and Jim Sheridan

Written By: Naomi Sheridan and Jim Sheridan

Color: Color

Length: 105 minutes

Language: English

Production Company: Fox Searchlight Pictures

Cast: Paddy Considine, Samantha Morton, Randall Carlton, Emma Bolger, Sarah Bolger, Neal Jones, Djimon Hounsou, and Juan Carlos Hernández

Film Synopsis

In America is about an Irish family who illegally immigrates to the United States and their struggles to survive in New York City. The film tells the story of Johnny (Paddy Considine), who is an aspiring actor with dreams of making it big, and how he and his wife Sarah (Samantha Morton) struggle to raise a family in America. *In America* was nominated three Academy Awards, including Best Screenplay and Best Actress (Samantha Morton).

MY FAMILY

(1995)

Genre: Drama

MPAA Rating: R

Alternative Title: *East L.A.*

Directed By: Gregory Nava

Produced By: Anna Thomas

Written By: Anna Thomas and Gregory Nava

Color: Color

Length: 128 minutes

Language: English

Production Company: American Playhouse

Cast: Edward James Olmos, Rafael Cortés, Evette Reina, Amelia Zapata, Jacob Vargas, Emilio Del Haro, Jennifer Lopez, and Esai Morales

Film Synopsis

My Family chronicles the events and tragedies of three generations of the Sanchez family, Mexican Americans that emigrated from Mexico and settled in Los Angeles. *My Family* was nominated for an Academy Award for Best Makeup.

UNDER THE SAME MOON

(2007)

Genre: Drama

MPAA Rating: PG-13

Alternative Title: *Bajo la Misma Luna*

Directed By: Patricia Riggen

Produced By: Gerardo Barrera, Lorenzo O'Brian, and Patricia Riggen

Written By: Ligiah Villalobos

Color: Color

Length: 106 minutes

Language: English

Production Company: Creando Films

Cast: Adrian Alonso, Kate Del Castillo, Eugenio Derbez, Maya Zapata, Carmen Salinas, Jesse Garcia, Angelina Peláez, and Gabriel Porras

Film Synopsis

Under the Same Moon is about the journey of a boy in search for his mother. The film tells the story of Carlitos (Adrian Alonso) who was living with his grandmother while his mother worked illegally in the United States. Carlitos's grandmother passes away, so he decides to embark on a journey to find his mother. The film depicts the events of Carlitos's journey as he illegally crosses the United States–Mexican border and attempts to survive in the search for his mother.

Labor Practices

Labor practices have been portrayed in films in various ways, including work environment, wages, employees, unions, and outsourcing. One issue relating to labor practices that is commonly depicted in numerous films throughout cinematic history are unions. From early depictions in *The Right to Strike* (1923) and *Give and Take* (1928), to Academy Award–winning depictions in *On the Waterfront* (1954), to more recent depictions in *Hoffa* (1992). Films relevant to labor practices can often pertain to other social issues such as consumerism. However, this social issue is handled separately in this chapter.

Other films dealing with labor practices not detailed in this volume include: *The $5.20 an Hour Dream* (1980), *Act of Vengeance* (1986), *American*

Dream (1990), *American Standoff* (2002), *The Angry Silence* (1960), *Black Fury* (1935), *Blood Feud* (1983), *Bostrobalikara: Garment Girls of Bangladesh* (2007), *Bread and Roses* (2000), *Comrades* (1986), *The Corporation* (2004), *Eila* (2003), *Entry Level* (2007), *The Fight in the Fields* (1997), *Friends and Enemies* (1987), *Germinal* (1993), *Gung Ho* (1986), *Harlan County U.S.A.* (1976), *Harlan County War* (2000), *Made in L.A.* (2007), *The Man in the White Suit* (1951), *The Molly Maguires* (1970), *My Cultural Divide* (2006), *Nalini by Day, Nancy by Night* (2005), *Net Worth* (1995), *Newsies* (1992), *Norma Rae* (1979), *North Country* (2005), *Ocean's Thirteen* (2007), *On the Waterfront* (1954), *Outsourced* (2006), *The Pajama Game* (1957), *The Price of Sugar* (2007), *Salt of the Earth* (1954), *The Stars Look Down* (1940), *Struggles in Steel: The Fight for Equal Opportunity* (1996), and *Tucker, the Man and his Dream* (1988).

10,000 BLACK MEN NAMED GEORGE

(2002)

Genre: Drama

MPAA Rating: R

Alternative Title: None

Directed By: Robert Townsend

Produced By: Michelle Mundy

Written By: Cyrus Nowrasteh

Color: Color

Length: 95 minutes

Language: English

Production Company: Dufferin Gate Productions

Cast: Andre Braugher, Charles S. Dutton, Mario Van Peebles, Brock Peters, Carla Brothers, Ellen Holly, Kedar Brown, and Collette Micks

Film Synopsis

10,000 Black Men Named George is set in America in the 1920s and tells the true story of A. Philip Randolph, a civil rights leader and union activist. The film depicts Randolph's (Andre Braugher) efforts to organize the black porters of the Pullman Rail Company into the Brotherhood of Sleeping Car Porters.

DAENS

(1993)

Genre: Biography

MPAA Rating: Not Rated

Alternative Title: *Priest Daens*

Directed By: Stijn Coninx

Produced By: Dirk Impens, Jean-Luc Ormières, Maria Peters, Hans Pos, and Dave Schram

Written By: François Chevallier

Color: Color

Length: 138 minutes

Language: Dutch, French, Latin, Spanish

Production Company: Favourite Films

Cast: Jan Decleir, Gérard Desarthe, Michael Pas, Antje de Boeck, Johan Leysen, Jappe Claes, Brit Alen, Wim Meuwissen, and Brenda Bertin

Film Synopsis

Daens is a biographical film based on the life of Father Adolf Daens. The film is set in Aalst during the 1890s and tells the true story of Daens (Jan Decleir), a Catholic priest in Belgium who fights to improve the horrific working conditions of the local factories. *Daens* was based on the novel, *Pieter Daens*, by Louis Paul Boon. The film was nominated for an Academy Award for Best Foreign Language Film.

HOFFA

(1992)

Genre: Biography

MPAA Rating: R

Alternative Title: None

Directed By: Danny DeVito

Produced By: Caldecot Chubb, Danny DeVito, and Edward R. Pressman

Written By: David Mamet

Color: Color

Length: 140 minutes

Language: English

Production Company: Twentieth Century-Fox Film Corporation

Cast: Jack Nicholson, Danny DeVito, John C. Reilly, Armand Assante, J.T. Walsh, Frank Whaley, John P. Ryan, Nicholas Pryor, and Karen Young

Film Synopsis

Hoffa is a biographical film based on the life of the legendary Teamster Union leader, Jimmy Hoffa (Jack Nicholson), from his early life in Michigan, to his leadership of the Teamsters Union, to his mysterious disappearance/death in 1975. The film was nominated for two Academy Awards for Best Makeup and Best Cinematography.

JOE HILL

(1971)

Genre: Drama

MPAA Rating: Not Rated

Alternative Title: *The Ballad of Joe Hill*

Directed By: Bo Widerberg

Produced By: Waldemar Bergendahl and Bo Widerberg

Written By: Steve Hopkins and Richard Weber

Color: Color

Length: 114 minutes

Language: English

Production Company: Bo Widerberg Film

Cast: Thommy Berggren, Anja Schmidt, Kevin Malave, Evert Anderson, Cathy Smith, David Moritz, Richard Weber, and Michael Logan

Film Synopsis

Joe Hill is a biographical film based on the life of Swedish-American labor activist Joe Hill. The film is set in the early 1900s and traces the life of Hill (Thommy Berggren) as he immigrates into the United States and fights for fair labor practices. The film highlights Hill's involvement with the Industrial Workers of the World and his connection, conviction, and execution for the murders of John and Arling Morrison.

MATEWAN

(1987)

Genre: Drama

MPAA Rating: PG-13

Alternative Title: None

Directed By: John Sayles

Produced By: Peggy Rajski and Maggie Renzi

Written By: John Sayles

Color: Color

Length: 135 minutes

Language: English

Production Company: Cinecom Entertainment Group

Cast: Chris Cooper, James Earl Jones, David Strathairn, Will Oldham, Mary McDonnell, Gordon Clapp, Kevin Tighe, and Bob Gunton

Film Synopsis

Matewan is based on the actual events surrounding the Battle of Matewan. The film is set in Matewan, West Virginia, in 1920. The film depicts the events of a coal miners' strike and their efforts to form a union, which eventually led to a shootout. *Matewan* was nominated for an Academy Award for Best Cinematography.

ROGER AND ME

(1989)

Genre: Documentary

MPAA Rating: R

Alternative Title: *A Humorous Look at How General Motors Destroyed Flint, Michigan*

Directed By: Michael Moore

Produced By: Michael Moore

Written By: Michael Moore

Color: Color

Length: 91 minutes

Language: English

Production Company: Dog Eat Dog Films

Cast: Michael Moore, James Bond, James Blanchard, Pat Boone, Timothy Jackson, Tom Kay, Karen Edgely, Anita Bryant, and Roger B. Smith

Film Synopsis

Roger & Me is a documentary that examines and explores General Motors CEO Robert Smith's decision to close several automobile manufacturing plants in Flint, Michigan. The film specifically focuses on the negative economic impact the downsizing had on the city and the nearly 30,000 people that lost their jobs because of the plant closings.

Media

Media and its depiction on film is a very common theme. This volume is focusing on media and its role. This includes unbiased reporting, sensationalism, manufacturing information and news, freedom of speech and press, and the role of media in society. Films relevant to media can often pertain to other social issues such as censorship. However, this social issue is handled separately in this chapter.

Other films dealing with media issues not detailed in this volume include: *Bowling for Columbine* (2002), *Broadcast News* (1987), *Choose Connor* (2007), *Don't Tell Me What to Think* (2008), *Enemy Image* (2005), *Fahrenheit 9/11* (2004), *The First Amendment Project: Fox vs. Franken* (2004), *Free Speech for Sale* (1999), *Frost/Nixon* (2008), *Live From Baghdad* (2002), *Manufacturing Consent: Noam Chomsky and the Media* (1992), *The Myth of the Liberal Media* (1998), *Only the News that Fits* (1989), *Orwell Rolls in His Grave* (2003), *Outfoxed: Rupert Murdoch's War on Journalism* (2004), *The Panama Deception* (1992), *Seeing is Believing: Handicams, Human Rights and the News* (2002), *Spin* (1995), *Talk to Me* (2007), *They Live* (1988), and *Winchell* (1998).

ALL THE PRESIDENT'S MEN

(1976)

Genre: Drama

MPAA Rating: PG

Alternative Title: None

Directed By: Alan J. Pakula

Produced By: Walter Coblenz

Written By: William Goldman

Color: Color

Length: 138 minutes

Language: English

Production Company: Warner Bros. Pictures

Cast: Dustin Hoffman, Robert Redford, Jack Warden, Jane Alexander, Ned Beatty, Meredith Baxter, Stephen Collins, and Jason Robards

Film Synopsis

All the President's Men is based on the actual events surrounding the Pulitzer Prize–winning investigative reporting of the Watergate scandal by Bob Woodward (Robert Redford) and Carl Bernstein (Dustin Hoffman) for the *Washington Post. All the President's Men* is based on the book by the same name written by Woodward and Bernstein. The film was nominated for eight Academy Awards, in which it won four, including Best Screenplay.

GOOD NIGHT, AND GOOD LUCK

(2005)

Genre: Drama

MPAA Rating: PG

Alternative Title: None

Directed By: George Clooney

Produced By: Grant Heslov

Written By: Grant Heslov and George Clooney

Color: Black and white

Length: 93 minutes

Language: English

Production Company: Warner Independent Pictures

Cast: Jeff Daniels, David Strathairn, Rose Abdoo, Alex Borstein, Peter Martin, Robert Downey Jr., George Clooney, and Reed Diamond

Film Synopsis

Good Night, and Good Luck is based on actual events and depicts the conflict between Edward R. Murrow and Senator Joseph McCarthy. Edward Murrow (David Strathairn) is a well-known radio and television journalist who questions Senator McCarthy's actions on the Senate Permanent Subcommittee on Investigations. *Good Night, and Good Luck* was nominated for six Academy Awards, including Best Picture, Best Director, and Best Screenplay.

MEDIUM COOL

(1969)

Genre: Drama

MPAA Rating: R

Alternative Title:

Directed By: Haskell Wexler

Produced By: Tully Friedman, Haskell Wexler, and Jerrold Wexler

Written By: Haskell Wexler

Color: Color

Length: 111 minutes

Language: English

Production Company: H & J

Cast: Robert Forster, Verna Bloom, Peter Bonerz, Sid McCoy, Marianna Hill, Harold Blankenship, Charles Geary, and Peter Boyle

Film Synopsis

Medium Cool is set in 1968 during the political and social unrest at the Democratic National Convention in Chicago. The film tells the story of a television cameraman, John Cassellis (Robert Forster), who uncovers that his news station is leaking information to the Federal Bureau of Investigation, and his relationship with a woman named Eileen (Verna Bloom) from a Chicago ghetto. The film was shot on location at the convention and combines fictional characters and actual events.

NETWORK

(1976)

Genre: Drama

MPAA Rating: R

Alternative Title: None

Directed By: Sidney Lumet

Produced By: Howard Gottfried

Written By: Paddy Chayefsky

Color: Color

Length: 121 minutes

Language: English

Production Company: Metro-Goldwyn-Mayer

Cast: Faye Dunaway, William Holden, Peter Finch, Robert Duvall, Ned Beatty, Arthur Burghardt, Wesley Addy, Kathy Cronkite, and Gene Gross

Film Synopsis

Network is a satirical film about a television network and their search for sensational news and shock video to increase ratings. The film tells the story of a veteran news anchor named Howard Beale (Peter Finch) who is fired because of declining ratings. In his last weeks of news broadcasts he goes on outrageous rants that increase ratings, eventually landing him his own television show where he tells viewers the outlandish and shocking truth. *Network* was nominated for 10 Academy Awards, in which it won Best Actor (Peter Finch), Best Actress (Faye Dunaway), Best Supporting Actress (Beatrice Straight), and Best Screenplay.

THANK YOU FOR SMOKING

(2006)

Genre: Comedy

MPAA Rating: R

Alternative Title: None

Directed By: Jason Reitman

Produced By: David O. Sacks

Written By: Jason Reitman

Color: Color

Length: 92 minutes

Language: English

Production Company: Room 9 Entertainment

Cast: Aaron Eckhart, David Koechner, William H. Macy, Katie Holmes, Adam Brody, Sam Elliott, and Rob Lowe

Film Synopsis

Thank You for Smoking tells the story of Nick Naylor (Aaron Eckhart), a tobacco lobbyist who uses various media outlets and public speeches to promote smoking and defend the rights of smokers. Nick starts a relationship with a young reporter named Heather Halloway (Katie Holmes), who uses the intimate details and secrets revealed to her by Nick in an article that depicts Nick as a horrific person. *Thank You for Smoking* is based on the book by the same name written by Christopher Buckley. The film was nominated for two Golden Globes for Best Actor (Aaron Eckhart) and Best Movie.

WMD: WEAPONS OF MASS DECEPTION

(2004)

Genre: Documentary

MPAA Rating: R

Alternative Title: None

Directed By: Danny Schechter

Produced By: Anna B. Pizarro

Written By: None Credited

Color: Color

Length: 98 minutes

Language: English

Production Company: Globalvision

Cast: Peter Arnett, George W. Bush, Dick Cheney, Maurice Hinchey, Tim Robbins, Bill O'Reilly, Nicholas Johnson, and Dan Rather

Film Synopsis

WMD: Weapons of Mass Deception is a documentary that examines and explores the media coverage surrounding the Iraq War. The film exposes the media's role in misleading the public with regard to the war in Iraq, specifically focusing on propaganda from the government and biased reporting by various media outlets.

Poverty

Poverty is a common element on the big screen. From poor orphans in *Oliver Twist* (1948) to Depression-era families in *Cinderella Man* (2005), poverty has been depicted in an array of styles. Films in this volume deal with poverty and its related issue of homelessness. Films relevant to poverty can often pertain to other social issues such as role of government. However, this social issue is handled separately in this chapter.

Other films dealing with poverty not detailed in this volume include: *Almost Home* (1995), *America's Invisible Children: The Homeless Education Crisis in America* (2007), *Born into Brothels* (2004), *By the Wayside* (2006), *Carissa* (2008), *Casa Libre/Freedom House* (2008), *Cathy Come Home* (1966), *The Children Nobody Wanted* (1981), *Children Underground* (2001), *City of God* (2002), *Coming to America* (1988), *Dark Days* (2000), *Devil Plays Hardball* (2006), *Dreams Don't Die* (1982), *Easy Street* (2006), *The End of Poverty?* (2008), *The Glass Wall* (1953), *God Bless the Child* (1988), *Good Will Hunting* (1997), *The Grapes of Wrath* (1940), *Hancock* (2008), *Have You Seen Clem* (2005), *Home Sweet Homeless* (1988), *Homeless `99* (1999), *Homeless Me* (2007), *Homeless Not Hopeless* (2007), *Humble Beauty: Skid Row Artists* (2008), *It Was a Wonderful Life* (1993), *The Jerk* (1979), *Katie Tippel* (1975), *Kids of the Majestic* (2008), *Life Below the Line: The World Poverty Crisis* (2007), *The Little Tramp* (1914), *Modern Time* (1936), *No Place Like Home* (1989), *Oliver Twist* (1948), *Poverty and Other Delights* (1996), *The Price of Sugar* (2007), *The Railway Children* (1970), *To Render a Life* (1992), *Samaritan: The Mitch Snyder Story* (1986), *Sense and Sensibility* (1995), *Sixth and Main* (1977), *The Soloist* (2009), *Stone Pillow* (1985), *Streetwise* (1984), *Sunshine Hotel* (2001), *Titanic* (1997), *Trading Places* (1983), *Union Square* (2003), and *With Honors* (1994).

AUGUST RUSH

(2007)

Genre: Drama

MPAA Rating: PG

Alternative Title: None

Directed By: Kirsten Sheriden

Produced By: Richard Barton Lewis

Written By: Nick Castle and James V. Hart

Color: Color

Length: 114 minutes

Language: English

Production Company: Warner Bros. Pictures

Cast: Freddie Highmore, Terrence Howard, Robin Williams,
 Jonathan Rhys Meyers, Keri Russell, William Sadler,
 Mykelti Williamson, and Ronald Guttman

Film Synopsis

August Rush is about an orphan and his quest to find his birth parents.
The film tells the story of Evan Taylor/August Rush (Freddie Highmore), a
poor orphan and musical prodigy. Evan works the streets of New York City
playing music and searching for his parents. *August Rush* was nominated
for an Academy Award for Best Original Song and for a Grammy Award for
Best Soundtrack.

CINDERELLA MAN

(2005)

Genre: Drama

MPAA Rating: PG-13

Alternative Title: None

Directed By: Ron Howard

Produced By: Brian Grazer, Ron Howard, and Penny Marshall

Written By: Cliff Hollingsworth

Color: Color

Length: 144 minutes

Language: English

Production Company: Universal Pictures

Cast: Russell Crowe, Renée Zellweger, Paul Giamatti, Paddy Considine,
 Craig Bierko, Bruce McGill, David Huband, Connor Price,
 and Patrick Lewis

Film Synopsis

Cinderella Man is based on the true story of Heavyweight Boxing Champion James Braddock (Russell Crowe) and his struggles to support his family during the Great Depression. The film highlights the Depression-era
boxer and his legendary comeback in which he defeated Max Baer to become the heavyweight champion. *Cinderella Man* was nominated for three
Academy Awards, including Best Supporting Actor (Paul Giamatti).

HOMELESS TO HARVARD: THE LIZ MURRAY STORY

(2003)

Genre: Biography

MPAA Rating: Not Rated

Alternative Title: None

Directed By: Peter Levin

Produced By: Michael Mahoney

Written By: Ronni Kern

Color: Color

Length: 104 minutes

Language: English

Production Company: Barnet Bain Films

Cast: Thora Birch, Michael Riley, Kelley Lynch, Robert Bockstael, Makyla Smith, Jennifer Pisana, Aron Tager, Marla McLean, and Ellen Page

Film Synopsis

Homeless to Harvard: The Liz Murray Story is a made-for-television film based on the powerful true story of Liz Murray. The film recounts Liz Murray's (Thora Birch) life and her relationship with her drug-addicted and HIV-infected parents, to her becoming homeless at age 15, and eventually being accepted into Harvard University. The film was nominated for three Emmy Awards, including Outstanding Actress (Thora Birch) and Outstanding Television Movie.

THE PURSUIT OF HAPPYNESS

(2006)

Genre: Biography/Drama

MPAA Rating: PG-13

Alternative Title: *The Pursuit of Happiness*

Directed By: Gabriele Muccino

Produced By: Jason Blumenthal, Todd Black, Will Smith, James Lassiter, and Steve Tisch

Written By: Steve Conrad

Color: Color

Length: 117 minutes

Language: English

Production Company: Columbia Pictures Corporation

Cast: Will Smith, Jaden Smith, Thandie Newton, Dan Castellaneta, Brian Howe, James Karen, Domenic Bove, and Kevin West

Film Synopsis

The Pursuit of Happyness is a biographical film about a homeless man named Chris Gardner who eventually becomes a financially stable stockbroker. The film chronicles the hardships Chris Gardner (Will Smith) and his son Christopher (Jaden Smith) endure, which ultimately lead to a better life for them. *The Pursuit of Happyness* was nominated for an Academy Award for Best Actor (Will Smith).

REVERSAL OF FORTUNE

(2005)

Genre: Documentary

MPAA Rating: Not Rated

Alternative Title: None

Directed By: Wayne Powers

Produced By: Leslie Garvin, Patty Ivins Specht, and Julie Pizzi

Written By: Robert DeMaio

Color: Color

Length: 68 minutes

Language: English

Production Company: PB & J Television

Cast: Ted Rodrigue

Film Synopsis

Reversal of Fortune is a documentary that attempts to answer the question, What would a homeless person do if he were given $100,000? The film chronicles Ted Rodrigue, a homeless man in Pasadena, California, and what he does with the money.

SLUMDOG MILLIONAIRE

(2008)

Genre: Drama

MPAA Rating: R

Alternative Title: None

Directed By: Danny Boyle

Produced By: Christian Colson

Written By: Simon Beaufoy

Color: Color

Length: 120 minutes

Language: English and Hindi

Production Company: Celador

Cast: Dev Patel, Anil Kapoor, Saurabh Shukla, Rajendranath Zutshi, Jeneva Talwar, Freida Pinto, and Irrfan Khan

Film Synopsis

Slumdog Millionaire is an epic story about a young man named Jamal (Dev Patel) from the slums of Mumbia, India, who appears on a trivia game show and surpasses everyone's expectations. The film tells the life story of Jamal through flashbacks and illustrates the horrific struggles and hardships he endured to survive the slums of Mumbia. *Slumdog Millionaire* was adapted for the screen from the book *Q and A* by Vikas Swarup. The film was nominated for 10 Academy Awards, in which it won eight including Best Picture, Best Director, Best Adapted Screenplay, Best Sound, Best Editing, and Best Cinematography.

Racism

Racism is a common theme in movies and has been depicted on the big screen throughout the history of cinema. Racism is simply the belief that one race is superior or inferior to another. Many films depict racism, the actions of racist individuals, and other discrimination-related beliefs and actions. Films relevant to racism can pertain to other social issues like gang violence, hate groups, and terrorism. However, these social issues are handled separately in this chapter.

Other films dealing with racism not detailed in this volume include the following: *Anti-Semitism in the 21st Century: The Resurgence* (2007), *The*

Autobiography of Miss Jane Pittman (1974), *The Believer* (2001), *Birth of a Nation* (1915), *Black Like Me* (1964), *Bridge of the Sun* (1961), *Cheyenne Autumn* (1964), *Crash* (2004), *The Crimson Kimono* (1960), *Crossfire* (1947), *Devils Doorway* (1950), *Driving Miss Daisy* (1989), *The Express* (2008), *Focus* (2001), *Freedom Writers* (2007), *Gentleman's Agreement* (1947), *The Glass Shield* (1994), *Glory Road* (2006), *Gran Torino* (2008), *The Great Debaters* (2007), *Guess Who's Coming to Dinner?* (1967), *Hairspray* (2007), *Harvest of Shame* (1960), *Holocaust* (1978), *In the Heat of the Night* (1967), *The Intruder* (1962), *Judge Horton and the Scottsboro Boys* (1976), *Lean on Me* (1989), *The Longest Hatred: The History of Anti-Semitism* (1993), *Monster's Ball* (2001), *No Way Out* (1950), *The Outsider* (1961), *The Pawnbroker* (1965), *Pleasantville* (1998), *Pride* (2007), *Remember the Titans* (2000), *Roots* (1977), *Roots: The Next Generation* (1979), *Seminole* (1953), *Skokie* (1981), *Stand and Deliver* (1987), *The Thin Blue Line* (1988), *A Time to Kill* (1996), *To Kill a Mockingbird* (1962), *Watermelon Man* (1970), and *When the Levies Broke: A Requiem in Four Acts* (2006).

AMERICAN HISTORY X

(1998)

Genre: Crime

MPAA Rating: R

Alternative Title: None

Directed By: Tony Kaye

Produced By: John Morrissey

Written By: David McKenna

Color: Color

Length: 119 minutes

Language: English

Production Company: New Line Cinema

Cast: Edward Norton, Edward Furlong, Beverly D'Angelo, Elliott Gould, Avery Brooks, Jennifer Lien, Fairuza Balk, Alex Sol, and Christopher Masterson

Film Synopsis

American History X tells the story of a racist neo-Nazi named Derek (Edward Norton) and his attempts to save his younger brother, Danny (Edward Furlong) from the same mistakes he made. Derek is sent to prison for killing two African Americans who tried to steal his truck and while he serves his time, he comes to the realization that racism is pointless. *American History X* was nominated for an Academy Award for Best Actor (Edward Norton).

DO THE RIGHT THING

(1989)

Genre: Comedy

MPAA Rating: R

Alternative Title: None

Directed By: Spike Lee

Produced By: Spike Lee

Written By: Spike Lee

Color: Color

Length: 120 minutes

Language: English

Production Company: 40 Acres & A Mule Filmworks

Cast: Danny Aiello, Ossie Davis, Ruby Dee, Spike Lee, Giancarlo Esposito, Richard Edson, John Turturro, John Savage, Martin Lawrence, and Samuel L. Jackson

Film Synopsis

Do the Right Thing is set in Brooklyn, New York, during the summer and depicts the events surrounding a multiracial conflict that ends in a race riot. The film was nominated for two Academy Awards, including Best Supporting Actor (Danny Aiello) and Best Screenplay.

GLORY

(1989)

Genre: Drama

MPAA Rating: R

Alternative Title: None

Directed By: Edward Zwick

Produced By: Freddie Fields

Written By: Kevin Jarre

Color: Color

Length: 122 minutes

Language: English

Production Company: TriStar Pictures

Cast: Matthew Broderick, Denzel Washington, Morgan Freeman, Cary Elwes, John Finn, Andre Braugher, and Keith Noble

Film Synopsis

Glory is based on the 54th Massachusetts Voluntary Infantry, which was the first entirely African American regiment of the Civil War. The film focuses on the regiment's commander, Robert Gould Shaw (Matthew Broderick) and the racism he and his regiment receive from both Union and Confederate armies. *Glory* was adapted from personal letters written by Robert Gould Shaw, *Lay This Laurel* by Lincoln Kirstein, and *One Gallant Rush* by Peter Burchard. The film was nominated for five Academy Awards, in which it won Best Supporting Actor (Denzel Washington), Best Sound, and Best Cinematography.

GRAN TORINO

(2008)

Genre: Crime

MPAA Rating: R

Alternative Title: None

Directed By: Clint Eastwood

Produced By: Clint Eastwood, Bill Gerber, and Robert Lorenz

Written By: Nick Schenk

Color: Color

Length: 116 minutes

Language: English

Production Company: Matten Productions

Cast: Clint Eastwood, Christopher Carley, Bee Hang, Ahney Her, Brian Haley, Geraldine Hughes, John Carroll Lynch, and Scott Eastwood

Film Synopsis

Gran Torino tells the story of Walt Kowalski (Clint Eastwood), a racist retired Korean War veteran and his struggles to accept his Hmong neighbors.

Walt slowly starts to build a relationship with his neighbors and attempts to help a teenage boy, Thao (Bee Vang), become an independent and confident young man. *Gran Torino* was nominated for a Golden Globe for Best Original Song.

MISSISSIPPI BURNING

(1988)

Genre: Crime

MPAA Rating: R

Alternative Title: None

Directed By: Alan Parker

Produced By: Robert F. Colesberry and Frederick Zollo

Written By: Chris Gerolmo

Color: Color

Length: 128 minutes

Language: English

Production Company: Orion Pictures Corporation

Cast: Gene Hackman, Willem Dafoe, Frances McDormand, Brad Dourif, R. Lee Ermey, Geoffrey Nauffts, Kevin Dunn, and Michael Rooker

Film Synopsis

Mississippi Burning is lossely based on the actual events surrounding the murders of three civil rights workers in Mississippi in 1964. The film tells the story of two FBI agents, Rupert Anderson (Gene Hackman) and Alan Ward (Willem Dafoe), who are investigating the murders and their struggles to uncover evidence and break the silence. *Mississippi Burning* was nominated for seven Academy Awards, in which it won Best Cinematography.

SEPARATE BUT EQUAL

(1991)

Genre: Drama

MPAA Rating: PG

Alternative Title: None

Directed By: George Stevens Jr.

Produced By: Stan Margulies and George Stevens Jr.

Written By: George Stevens Jr.

Color: Color

Length: 186 minutes

Language: English

Production Company: George Stevens Productions

Cast: Sidney Poitier, Burt Lancaster, Cleavon Little, Richard Kiley, Macon McCalman, Gloria Foster, Randle Mell, and John Rothman

Film Synopsis

Separate by Equal is a made-for-television film based on the landmark Supreme Court case, *Brown v. Board of Education.* The film recounts the Court case and the final ruling, which would become the first major victory for the Civil Rights movement and would help end racial segregation. *Separate but Equal* was nominated for eight Emmy Awards, in which it won two, including Outstanding Drama.

Religion

Religion is one of the most controversial social issues currently in society. The issue divides individuals into various religions, which can be divided into different religious groups, which can be divided into various denominations or sects, which also can be divided. Although many individuals have strong beliefs regarding religion, it is still a popular topic. Films relevant to various religious topics can often pertain to other social issues, which are supported or denied based on the beliefs of a specific religion. The majority of films pertained in the volume are related to the five major world religions (Buddhism, Christianity, Hinduism, Islam, and Judaism). Films dealing with religion can be viewed as (1) films about religion or about a religious event, person, belief, etc., or (2) films that deal with religion as part of the plot or of a character.

Other films dealing with religion not detailed in this volume include: *The Apostle* (1997), *Battle for the Minds* (1996), *Chasing Buddha* (2000), *Church vs. State* (1998), *The Crucible* (1996), *The Cup* (2000), *Divorcing God* (2009), *Earth* (1998), *Fall From Grace* (2007), *For the Bible Tells Me So* (2007), *In God We Tru$t* (1980), *Inherit the Wind* (1960), *Jesus Camp* (2006), *Jesus Christ Superstar* (1973), *Judgment* (2001), *Keeping the Faith* (2000), *Kingdom of Heaven* (2005), *The Kite Runner* (2007), *The Last Emperor* (1987), *Leap of Faith* (1992), *Life Brian* (1979), *The Lion of the Desert* (1980), *Little Buddha* (1993), *Luther* (2003), *Mary* (2005), *The Mission* (1986), *Muhammad: The Last Proph-*

et (2002), *My Son the Fanatic* (1997), *Nazrah: A Muslim Women's Perspective* (2003), *Paradise* (2004), *The Passion of the Christ* (2004), *The Prince of Egypt* (1998), *The Prosecutor* (1983), *Religion, Inc.* (1989), *Religulous* (2008), *Saved!* (2004), *Soul Searching* (2007), *There Will Be Blood* (2007), and *Yentl* (1983).

GANDHI

(1982)

Genre: Biography

MPAA Rating: PG

Alternative Title: *Richard Attenborough's Film: Gandhi*

Directed By: Richard Attenborough

Produced By: Richard Attenborough

Written By: John Briley

Color: Black and white/Color

Length: 188 minutes

Language: English

Production Company: Carolina Bank

Cast: Ben Kingsley, Candice Bergen, Martin Sheen, John Gielgud, Edward Fox, Trevor Howard, John Mills, and Saeed Jaffrey

Film Synopsis

Gandhi is a biographical account of the life of Mahatma Gandhi, a lawyer who became a major political and spiritual leader of India. *Gandhi* won eight Academy Awards, including Best Picture, Best Actor (Ben Kingsley), Best Screenplay, and Best Director.

KUNDUN

(1997)

Genre: Drama/Biography

MPAA Rating: PG-13

Alternative Title: None

Directed By: Martin Scorsese

Produced By: Barbara De Fina

Written By: Melissa Mathison

Color: Color

Length: 134 minutes

Language: English/Tibetan/Mandarin

Production Company: De Fina-Cappa

Cast: Tenzin Thuthob Tsarong, Gyurme Tethong, Tulku Jamyang
    Kunga Tenzin, and Tenzin Yeshi Paichang

Film Synopsis

Kundun is based on the life of the spiritual leader of Tibet, the Dalai
Lama. The film chronicles the events of the fourteenth Dalai Lama and his
life between 1937 and 1959, highlighting his selection to be the Dalai Lama
to his exile from Tibet in 1959. The film was nominated for four Academy
Awards, including Best Cinematography and Best Costume Design.

THE LAST TEMPTATION OF CHRIST

(1988)

Genre: Drama

MPAA Rating: R

Alternative Title: *Passion*

Directed By: Martin Scorsese

Produced By: Barbara De Fina

Written By: Paul Schrader

Color: Color

Length: 164 minutes

Language: English

Production Company: Cineplex-Odeon Films

Cast: Willem Dafoe, Harvey Keitel, Paul Greco, Steve Shill,
    Barbara Hershey, Verna Bloom, Victor Argo, Paul Herman,
    and Michael Been

Film Synopsis

The Last Temptation of Christ tells the story of Jesus Christ and the struggles he endured as a human. The film focuses on Jesus's temptations of sin
and how he overcame the temptations he faced. *The Last Temptation of Christ*
was based on the book by the same name written by Nikos Kazantzakis. The
film was nominated for an Academy Award for Best Director.

THE MESSAGE

(1976)

Genre: Biography

MPAA Rating: PG

Alternative Title: *Mohammed, Messenger of God*

Directed By: Moustapha Akkad

Produced By: Moustapha Akkad

Written By: H.A.L. Craig, Tewfik El-Hakim, A.B. Jawdat El-Sahhar, A.B. Rahman El-Sharkawi, and Mohammad Ali Maher

Color: Color

Length: 177 minutes

Language: English

Production Company: Filmco International Productions

Cast: Anthony Quinn, Irene Pappas, Michael Ansara, Johnny Sekka, Michael Forest, Damien Thomas, Ahmed Abdelhalim, and John Bennett

Film Synopsis

The Message is based on the central figure of Islam and messenger of God, Muhammad. The film depicts the life of Muhammad and highlights key events throughout his journey to being named the Prophet of Islam. The film is told from the perspectives of various individuals including his uncle, Hamza (Anthony Quinn). The film was nominated for an Academy Award for Best Original Score.

SIDDHARTHA

(1972)

Genre: Drama

MPAA Rating: R

Alternative Title: None

Directed By: Conrad Brooks

Produced By: Conrad Rooks

Written By: Conrad Brooks, Natasha Ullman, and Paul Mayersberg

Color: Color

Length: 89 minutes

Language: English

Production Company: Lotus Films

Cast: Shashi Kapoor, Simi Garwal, Romesh Sharma, Pinchoo Kappoor, Zul Vellani, Kumal Kappoor, and Holy Sadhus of Rishikesh

Film Synopsis

Siddhartha is based on the novel by the same name written by Herman Hesse. The film is set in the time of Buddha and follows Siddhartha (Shashi Kapoor) as he embarks on a journey in search of enlightenment.

THE TEN COMMANDMENTS

(1956)

Genre: Adventure

MPAA Rating: G

Alternative Title: None

Directed By: Cecil B. DeMille

Produced By: Cecil B. DeMille

Written By: Jesse Lasky Jr., Jack Gariss, and Fredric M. Frank

Color: Color

Length: 220 minutes

Language: English

Production Company: Motion Picture Associates

Cast: Charlton Heston, Yul Brynner, Anne Baxter, Edward G. Robinson, Yvonne De Carlo, John Derek, Debra Paget, and Nina Foch

Film Synopsis

The Ten Commandments is an epic film about the life of Moses. The film recounts Moses' (Charlton Heston) life, focusing on his early adulthood and his relationship with his adopted brother, Prince Rameses II (Yul Brynner), and Princess Nefretiri (Anne Baxter). The film was nominated for seven Academy Awards, in which it won Best Special Effects.

Role of Government

The role of government is a social issue that is often depicted in films. Role of government, simply put, is the role and/or power of the government, its agencies, and its officials have over the populous and the world. Many films depict the role of government as a "Big Brother" mentality. Some argue that this issue is divided into those who want more government and those who want less government. Films relevant to the role of government can often pertain to other social issues such as gun control, abortion, terrorism, censorship, immigration, etc. However, these social issues are handled separately in this chapter.

Other films dealing with the role of government not detailed in this volume include: *An American President* (1995), *Brave New World* (1998), *A Clockwork Orange* (1971), *Dave* (1993), *Dr. Strangelove or: How I Learned to Stop Worrying and Love the Bomb* (1964), *Elizabeth* (1998), *Endgame: Blueprint for Global Enslavement* (2007), *Equilibrium* (2002), *Fahrenheit 9/11* (2004), *The Fog of War* (2003), *Good Night, and Good Luck* (2005), *I, Robot* (2004), *Julius Caesar* (1953), *Martial Law 9/11: Rise of the Police State* (2005), *Mastergate* (1992), *Minority Report* (2002), *Nixon* (1995), *Rendition* (2007), *Shadow on the Land* (1968), *Shooter* (2007), *Spy Game* (2001), *Star Wars* (1977), *TerrorStorm: A History of Government-Sponsored Terrorism* (2006), *The Trials of Henry Kissinger* (2002), *Triumph of the Will* (1935), *The U.S. vs. John Lennon* (2006), and *War Games* (1983).

1984

(1956)

Genre: Drama

MPAA Rating: Not Rated

Alternative Title: None

Directed By: Michael Anderson

Produced By: N. Peter Rathvon

Written By: Ralph Gilbert Bettison

Color: Black and white

Length: 90 minutes

Language: English

Production Company: Holiday Film Productions Ltd.

Cast: Edmond O'Brien, Michael Redgrave, David Kossoff, Jan Sterling, Donald Pleasence, Mervyn Johns, and Michael Ripper

Film Synopsis

1984 tells the story of a civil servant named Winston Smith (Edmond O'Brien) in a futuristic totalitarian society. The film depicts Winston's life as he grows restless and starts to rebel against Big Brother. *1984* is based on the novel by the same name written by George Orwell.

CHARLIE WILSON'S WAR

(2007)

Genre: Biography/Drama

MPAA Rating: R

Alternative Title: None

Directed By: Mike Nichols

Produced By: Gary Goetzman and Tom Hanks

Written By: Aaron Sorkin

Color: Color

Length: 102 minutes

Language: English

Production Company: Universal Pictures

Cast: Tom Hanks, Amy Adams, Julia Roberts, Philip Seymour Hoffman, Hilary Angelo, Jud Taylor, Kirby Mitchell, and Rachel Nichols

Film Synopsis

Charlie Wilson's War is a biographical film about Charlie Wilson, a U.S. Congressman from Texas. The film recounts Wilson's (Tom Hanks) involvement in the covert operation known as Operation Cyclone, which organized the Afghan Mujahideen against the Soviet Union. The film was adapted for the big screen from the book *Charlie Wilson's War: The Extraordinary Story of the Largest Covert Operation in History* written by George Crile. The film was nominated for an Academy Award for Best Supporting Actor (Philip Seymour Hoffman).

ENEMY OF THE STATE

(1998)

Genre: Action

MPAA Rating: R

Alternative Title: None

Directed By: Tony Scott

Produced By: Jerry Bruckheimer

Written By: David Marconi

Color: Color

Length: 132 minutes

Language: English

Production Company: Touchstone Pictures

Cast: Will Smith, Gene Hackman, Jon Voight, Lisa Bonet, Regina King, Barry Pepper, Laura Cayouette, and Stuart Wilson

Film Synopsis

Enemy of the State tells the story of a lawyer named Robert Dean (Will Smith) and his thrilling journey while being hunted by National Security agents. Dean accidentally receives evidence depicting the murder of a congressman and the government official responsible will stop at nothing to seize and destroy the evidence.

MR. SMITH GOES TO WASHINGTON

(1939)

Genre: Drama

MPAA Rating: Not Rated

Alternative Title: *Frank Capra's Mr. Smith Goes to Washington*

Directed By: Frank Capra

Produced By: Frank Capra

Written By: Sidney Buchman

Color: Black and white

Length: 129 minutes

Language: English

Production Company: Columbia Pictures Corporation

Cast: Jean Arthur, James Stewart, Edward Arnold, Claude Rains, Guy Kibbee, Eugene Pallette, Thomas Mitchell, H.B. Warner, and Grant Mitchell

Film Synopsis

Mr. Smith Goes to Washington tells the story of Jefferson Smith (James Stewart), who is appointed by the governor to fill the state's vacant U.S.

Senate seat. Once Mr. Smith arrives in Washington, his political and ethical beliefs collide with corrupt politicians who attempt to manipulate him. *Mr. Smith Goes to Washington* is based on the unpublished story written by Lewis Foster. The film was nominated for 11 Academy Awards, in which it won Best Writing.

V FOR VENDETTA

(2005)

Genre: Action

MPAA Rating: R

Alternative Title: None

Directed By: James McTeigue

Produced By: Grant Hill, Joel Silver, Andy Wachowski, and Larry Wachowski

Written By: Andy Wachowski and Larry Wachowski

Color: Color

Length: 132 Minutes

Language: English

Production Company: Silver Pictures

Cast: Natalie Portman, Hugo Weaving, John Hurt, Stephen Rea, Stephen Fry, Tim Pigott-Smith, Ben Miles, Rupert Graves, and Roger Allam

Film Synopsis

V for Vendetta is set in totalitarian Britain in 2038, which is ruled by the Far-Right Norsefire regime. The film tells the story of V (Hugo Weaving) and his relationship with Evey (Natalie Portman) and his continuous battle against the corrupt totalitarian government in power. *V for Vendetta* was adapted for the big screen from the graphic novel by the same name written by David Lloyd and Alan Moore.

WACO: THE RULES OF ENGAGEMENT

(1997)

Genre: Documentary

MPAA Rating: Not Rated

Alternative Title: None

Directed By: William Gazecki

Produced By: William Gazecki and Michael McNulty

Written By: William Gazecki, Dan Gifford, and Michael McNulty

Color: Color

Length: 165 minutes

Language: English

Production Company: Fifth Estate Productions

Cast: Dan Gifford, Clive Doyle, Jack Harwell, Dick J. Reavis,
    James D. Tabor, and Joe Biden

Film Synopsis

Waco: The Rules of Engagement is a documentary that recounts the events
surrounding the 1993 conflict between Branch Davidians and the FBI and
ATF in Waco, Texas. The film focuses on the conflict and the role the United States government played in the destruction of the compound and the
deaths of 76 Branch Davidians, including 21 children. The film was nominated for an Academy Award for Best Documentary.

School Violence

School violence has been depicted on-screen in various forms throughout cinematic history. Traditionally school violence has taken the form of
school bullying or physical fighting. More recently, depictions of school
violence have transformed into more serious infractions like school shoot-
ings. The films discussed in this volume focuses on school violence, which
entails bullying, fighting, and assault with weapons. Films relevant to this
topic can often pertain to other social issues, such as racism, hate groups,
gun control, and gang violence. However, these social issues are handled
separately in this chapter.

Other films dealing with school violence not detailed in this volume
include the following: *American Gun* (2005), *Carrie* (1976), *Detention: The
Siege at Johnson High* (1997), *Duck! The Columbine High Massacre* (1999), *Hid-
den Rage* (2008), *Higher Learning* (1995), *Home Room* (2002), *Klass* (2007),
Massacre at Virginia Tech (2008), *Powder* (1995), *Razone* (2006), *School Ties*
(1992), *Silence of Fear* (2000), *Students vs. School Violence* (2000), and *Teen
Truth: An Inside Look at Bullying and School Violence* (2006).

AMERICAN YEARBOOK

(2004)

Genre: Romance

MPAA Rating: Not Rated

Alternative Title: None

Directed By: Brian Ging

Produced By: Jason F. Brown and Brian Ging

Written By: Brian Ging

Color: Color

Length: 97 minutes

Language: English

Production Company: All Planet Studios

Cast: Nick Tagas, Jon Carlo Alvarez, Giovannie Espiritu, Chris Ratti, Ryon Nixon, Matthew Gudenius, Jennifer Noble, Daniel Timko, and Eric Nygard

Film Synopsis

American Yearbook tells the story of Will Nash (Nick Tagas), a typical high school student that is constantly being bullied by Ian (Chris Ratti) and Jason (Ryon Nixon). Will finally gets tired of being bullied and decides to get revenge against Ian and Jason.

BANG BANG YOU'RE DEAD

(2002)

Genre: Drama

MPAA Rating: R

Alternative Title: None

Directed By: Guy Ferland

Produced By: Deboragh Gabler and Paul Hellerman

Written By: William Mastrosimone

Color: Color

Length: 87 minutes

Language: English

Production Company: Every Guy Productions

Cast: Thomas Cavanagh, Ben Foster, Janel Moloney, Randy Harrison, Jane McGregor, Eric Johnson, David Paetkau, and Brent Glenen

Film Synopsis

Bang Bang You're Dead is a made-for-television film that tells the story of Trevor (Ben Foster), a troubled and misunderstood high school student who is constantly bullied by a group of students called Trogs. Eventually the bullying sends Trevor over the edge and he plans to commit a serious act of violence.

BOWLING FOR COLUMBINE

(2002)

Genre: Documentary

MPAA Rating: R

Alternative Title: None

Directed By: Michael Moore

Produced By: Jim Czarnecki, Charles Bishop, Michael Moore, Michael Donovan, and Kathleen Glynn

Written By: Michael Moore

Color: Color

Length: 120 minutes

Language: English

Production Company: Alliance Atlantis Communications

Cast: Michael Moore, Jacobo Arbenz, George W. Bush, Dick Clark, Arthur Busch, Mike Epstein, Charlton Heston, Jimmie Hughes, and Dick Hurlin

Film Synopsis

Bowling for Columbine is a documentary that examines and explores the Columbine High School massacre. The film focuses on possible causes and examines school violence and the nature of violence in the United States. *Bowling for Columbine* won an Academy Award for Best Documentary Film.

ELEPHANT

(2003)

Genre: Crime

MPAA Rating: R

Alternative Title: None

Directed By: Gus Van Sant

Produced By: Dany Wolf

Written By: Gus Van Sant

Color: Color

Length: 81 minutes

Language: English

Production Company: HBO Films

Cast: Alex Frost, Eric Deulen, John Robinson, Elias McConnell, Jordan Taylor, Timothy Bottoms, Carrie Finklea, and Ellis Williams

Film Synopsis

Elephant portrays the lives of several high school students as they go about their days, unaware of the school shooting that is about to take place. The film depicts the events before, during, and after the school shooting. The film is partly based on the 1999 Columbine High School massacre.

RATS AND BULLIES

(2004)

Genre: Documentary

MPAA Rating: Not Rated

Alternative Title: *Rats and Bullies: The Dawn-Marie Wesley Story*

Directed By: Ray Buffer and Roberta McMillan

Produced By: Ray Buffer and Roberta McMillan

Written By: Ray Buffer and Roberta McMillan

Color: Color

Length: 102 minutes

Language: English

Production Company: R&R Media Productions

Cast: Roberta McMillan, Cindy Wesley, Kyla Mae Dunn, Rosalind Wiseman, Daniel Wesley, Randy Hawes, Karen McQuade, and Lee Hanlon

Film Synopsis

Rats and Bullies is a documentary that explores and examines school bullying, retaliation, suicide, and accountability. The film focuses on the story of Dawn-Marie Wesley, a 14-year-old girl who committed suicide because she was being bullied and terrorized by three girls from her school. The girls were named in the suicide note and were eventually held accountable in a court of law.

ZERO DAY

(2003)

Genre: Drama

MPAA Rating: PG-13

Alternative Title: None

Directed By: Ben Coccio

Produced By: Ben Coccio

Written By: Ben Coccio and Christopher Coccio

Color: Color

Length: 92 minutes

Language: English

Production Company: Professor Bright Films

Cast: Andre Keuck, Cal Robertson, Rachel Benichak, Christopher Coccio, Gerhard Keuck, and Johanne Keuck

Film Synopsis

Zero Day tells the story of two high school students, Andre (Andre Keuck) and Cal (Cal Robertson), who are fed up with school and all of their classmates. Andre and Cal decide to plan a horrific attack on their school. As the plan moves closer to implementation, they decide to keep a video diary, where they share their feelings and ideas about the plan.

Spousal Abuse

Spousal abuse is most often defined as the verbal, physical, emotional, psychological, and/or sexual maltreatment of a spouse. Spousal abuse has often been depicted on film throughout the history of cinema. Over the last 30–40 years spousal abuse has become a more central theme of films. Films relevant to spousal abuse can often pertain to other social issues, such as divorce and women's rights. However, these social issues are handled separately in this chapter.

Other films depicting spousal abuse not detailed in this volume include: *Battered* (1978), *Before Woman Had Wings* (1997), *Black and Blue* (1999), *Caught* (1949), *China Moon* (1994), *The Conviction of Kitty Dodds* (1993), *Diary of a Mad Housewife* (1970), *Foolish Wives* (1922), *The Golden Chance* (1915), *Greed* (1925), *Hearts of the World* (1918), *House of Secrets* (1993), *If Someone Had Known* (1995), *Intimate Strangers* (1971), *Mortal Thoughts* (1991), *Not Without My Daughter* (1991), *Once Were Warriors* (1994), *Personal Vendetta* (1995), *The Quiet Room* (1996), *Raging Bull* (1980), *Sleeping with the Devil* (1997), *Sling Blade* (1996), *Take My Eyes* (2003), *Unforgivable* (1996), *What's Love Got to Do with It* (1993), and *Woman on the Beach* (1947).

A CRY FOR HELP: THE TRACEY THURMAN STORY

(1989)

Genre: Drama

MPAA Rating: Not Rated

Alternative Title: *Under the Law: The Tracey Thurman Story*

Directed By: Robert Markowitz

Produced By: Lee Miller

Written By: Beth Sullivan

Color: Color

Length: 96 minutes

Language: English

Production Company: Dick Clark Productions

Cast: Nancy McKeon, Dale Midkiff, Graham Jarvis, Philip Baker Hall, Yvette Heyden, Seth Isler, David Ciminello, and Madison Mason

Film Synopsis

A Cry for Help: The Tracey Thurman Story is a made-for-television film that tells the tragic story of Tracey Thurman (Nancy McKeon), a Connecticut housewife and continuous victim of domestic abuse at the hands of her husband, Buck (Dale Midkiff). Eventually Buck's rage culminates one night and he stabs Tracey 13 times. Tracey barely survives and sues the local law enforcement for not providing her with appropriate protection. The film was nominated for an Emmy Award for Best Makeup.

THE BURNING BED

(1984)

Genre: Drama

MPAA Rating: Not Rated

Alternative Title: None

Directed By: Robert Greenwald

Produced By: Carol Schreder

Written By: Rose Leiman Goldemberg

Color: Color

Length: 95 minutes

Language: English

Production Company: Tisch/Avnet Productions Inc.

Cast: Farrah Fawcett, Paul Le Mat, Richard Masur, Christa Denton, Grace Zabriskie, Heather Rich, Penelope Milford, and James T. Callahan

Film Synopsis

The Burning Bed is a made-for-television film that recounts the actions of Francine Hughes, an abused housewife (Farrah Fawcett), who, after 13 years of domestic abuse, set her husband on fire while he slept. The film was adapted from the book by the same name, written by Faith McNulty. *The Burning Bed* was nominated for three Golden Globes, in which it won Best Supporting Actor (Paul Le Mat).

THE PERFECT HUSBAND

(2004)

Genre: Drama

MPAA Rating: R

Alternative Title: *The Perfect Spouse*

Directed By: Douglas Jackson

Produced By: Neil Bregman and Stefan Wodoslawsky

Written By: Ken Sanders and George Saunders

Color: Color

Length: 94 minutes

Language: English

Production Company: Movie Venture 2 Inc.

Cast: Tracy Nelson, Michael Riley, Thomas Calabro, Andrea Roth, Steve Adams, and Sophie Gendron

Film Synopsis

The Perfect Husband tells the story of Lisa (Tracy Nelson) and Ty (Michael Riley) and their blissful relationship and marriage. However, the happiness wears off and Lisa's life becomes a nightmare. Ty becomes controlling and jealous of anything intruding on their life, eventually leading him to make Lisa a prisoner.

SHATTERED DREAMS

(1990)

Genre: Drama

MPAA Rating: Not Rated

Alternative Title: None

Directed By: Robert Iscove

Produced By: Stephanie Austin

Written By: David Hill

Color: Color

Length: 94 minutes

Language: English

Production Company: Carolco Pictures

Cast: Lindsay Wagner, Michael Nouri, James Karen, Georgann Johnson, Ken Jenkins, Irene Miracle, Bryan Clark, Jay R. Ferguson, and Patricia Heaton

Film Synopsis

Shattered Dreams is a made-for-television film that tells the story of a housewife named Charlotte (Lindsay Wagner) who finds out that her marriage is not a fairytale after all. Charlotte's husband, John (Michael Nouri), is a powerful attorney who physically and mentally abuses her. She endures John's abuse for 18 years until she finally finds the strength to leave him.

SLEEPING WITH THE ENEMY

(1991)

Genre: Drama

MPAA Rating: R

Alternative Title: None

Directed By: Joseph Ruben

Produced By: Leonard Goldberg

Written By: Ronald Bass

Color: Color

Length: 90 minutes

Language: English

Production Company: Twentieth Century-Fox Film Corporation

Cast: Julia Roberts, Patrick Bergin, Kevin Anderson, Elizabeth Lawrence, Kyle Secor, Claudette Nevins, Harley Venton, Sandi Shackelford, and Nancy Fish

Film Synopsis

Sleeping with the Enemy tells the story of Laura Burney (Julia Roberts), who is married to an obsessive and abusive husband, Martin Burney (Patrick Bergin). Laura fakes her own death to escape from Martin. She moves to a small town and meets a man named Ben Woodward (Kevin Anderson), only to find out her husband is aware of her hoax and is not happy. *Sleeping with the Enemy* was adapted for the screen from the book by the same name written by Nancy Price.

UNFORGIVABLE

(1996)

Genre: Drama

MPAA Rating: R

Alternative Title: None

Directed By: Graeme Campbell

Produced By: Joan Barnett and Jack Grossbart

Written By: Adam Rodman

Color: Color

Length: 120 minutes

Language: English

Production Company: Brayton-Carlucci Productions

Cast: John Ritter, Kevin Dunn, Harley Jane Kozak, Gina Philips, Susan Gibney, Mariangela Pino, Steven Anderson, James McDaniel, and Michael Flynn

Film Synopsis

Unforgivable is a made-for-television film about a man named Paul Hegstrom (John Ritter). Paul is a family man who physically abuses his wife and emotionally abuses his children. He eventually leaves his wife and gets a new girlfriend. However, in a fit of rage, he almost kills her and is ordered to get professional help.

Teen Pregnancy

Teen pregnancy has been depicted on the big screen throughout cinematic history. Teen pregnancy typically refers to any female 19 years old or younger becoming pregnant. It is said that three out of every ten teenage girls will get pregnant. Traditional teen pregnancy films closely explore other social issues such as abortion and women's rights. However, these social issues are handled separately in this chapter. Oftentimes, teen pregnancy films have a happy ending, limiting the depiction of teen pregnancy as a social dilemma.

Other films depicting teen pregnancy not detailed in this volume include: *Amanda Fallon* (1973), *American Girl* (2002), *Blue Denim* (1959), *Cry-Baby* (1990), *Daddy* (1987), *The Doctor Is In: Teen Pregnancy* (1990), *Fifteen and Pregnant* (1998), *For Keeps* (1988), *The Girls of Huntington House* (1973), *I Want to Keep My Baby* (1976), *Manny & Lo* (1996), *Mr. and Mrs. Bo Jo Jones* (1971), *Sugar & Spice* (2001), *A Taste of Honey* (1961), *Teenage Mother* (1967), and *Where the Heart Is* (2000).

COAL MINER'S DAUGHTER

(1980)

Genre: Biography/Drama

MPAA Rating: PG

Alternative Title: None

Directed By: Michael Apted

Produced By: Bernard Schwartz

Written By: Thomas Rickman

Color: Color

Length: 125 minutes

Language: English

Production Company: Universal Pictures

Cast: Sissy Spacek, Tommy Lee Jones, Phyllis Boyens, Levon Helm, Billy Anderson Jr., Foister Dickerson, Malla McCown, and Pamela McCown

Film Synopsis

Coal Miner's Daughter is a biographical film about the life of country music singer Loretta Lynn. The film recounts the life of Loretta Lynn (Sissy Spacek), who came from a poor family, was married at age 13, and by 18 had four children. Loretta began singing country music and quickly became its first female star. *Coal Miner's Daughter* was adapted for the screen from her autobiography by the same name. The film was nominated for seven Academy Awards, in which it won Best Actress (Sissy Spacek).

JUNO

(2007)

Genre: Comedy

MPAA Rating: PG-13

Alternative Title: None

Directed By: Jason Reitman

Produced By: Lianne Halfon, John Malkovich, Mason Novick, and Russell Smith

Written By: Diablo Cody

Color: Color

Length: 96 minutes

Language: English

Production Company: Dancing Elk Productions

Cast: Ellen Page, Michael Cera, Jennifer Garner, Jason Bateman, Allison Janney, J.K. Simmons, Olivia Thirlby, Rainn Wilson, and Darla Vandenbossche

Film Synopsis

Juno tells the story of a 16-year-old girl name Juno (Ellen Page) who is faced with an unplanned pregnancy. The film focuses on Juno's life as a pregnant teenager and on her decision to have the baby and give it up for adoption. *Juno* was nominated for four Academy Awards, in which it won Best Screenplay.

MOM AT SIXTEEN

(1998)

Genre: Drama

MPAA Rating: Not Rated

Alternative Title: *Just a Baby*

Directed By: Peter Werner

Produced By: Frank von Zerneck, Robert M. Sertner, and Bernard Sofronski

Written By: Nancey Silvers

Color: Color

Length: 86 minutes

Language: English

Production Company: Von Zerneck Sertner Films

Cast: Danielle Panabaker, Clare Stone, Jane Krakowski, Tyler Hynes, Colin Ferguson, Mercedes Ruehl, Megan Edwards, and Rejean Cournoyer

Film Synopsis

Mom at Sixteen is a made-for-television film about 16-year-old Jacey (Danielle Panabaker), who unexpectedly becomes a mother. Jacey's mother convinces her to keep the birth a secret; however, one of her teachers uncovers the truth. Jacey then decides to put the baby up for adoption.

RIDING IN CARS WITH BOYS

(2001)

Genre: Biography

MPAA Rating: PG-13

Alternative Title: None

Directed By: Penny Marshall

Produced By: Julie Ansell, James L. Brooks, Sara Colleton, Laurence Mark, and Richard Sakai

Written By: Morgan Ward

Color: Color

Length: 132 minutes

Language: English

Production Company: Gracie Films

Cast: Drew Barrymore, Steve Zahn, Adam Garcia, Brittany Murphy, Lorraine Bracco, James Woods, Rosie Perez, Peter Facinelli, and Sara Gilbert

Film Synopsis

Riding in Cars with Boys is based on the true story of Beverly D'Onofrio. The film recounts the life of Beverly (Drew Barrymore) and focuses on her teen pregnancy and failed marriage. It portrays Beverly's life struggles and how she overcame them to eventually earn a master's degree. The film is based on Beverly D'Onofrio's autobiography by the same name.

SAVED!

(2004)

Genre: Comedy

MPAA Rating: PG-13

Alternative Title: None

Directed By: Brian Dannelly

Produced By: Michael Ohoven, Sandy Stern, Michael Stipe, and William Vince

Written By: Brian Dannelly and Michael Urban

Color: Color

Length: 92

Language: English

Production Company: United Artists

Cast: Jena Malone, Mandy Moore, Macaulay Culkin, Patrick Fugit,
Heather Matarazzo, Eva Amurri, Mary-Louise Parker,
and Martin Donovan

Film Synopsis

Saved! is a satirical comedy about teenage life, religion, and pregnancy.
The film tells the story of Mary (Jena Malone) who receives a vision from
God telling her to have sex with her boyfriend, Dean (Chad Faust), to help
prevent him from becoming gay. Mary then becomes pregnant. As a pregnant teenager she is ridiculed and ostracized by friends and family. In the
process she finds new friends and a new perspective on life.

TOO YOUNG TO BE A DAD

(2002)

Genre: Drama

MPAA Rating: Not Rated

Alternative Title: *A Family's Decision*

Directed By: Éva Gárdos

Produced By: Michael Mahoney

Written By: Edithe Swensen

Color: Color

Length: 120 minutes

Language: English

Production Company: Lifetime Television

Cast: Kathy Baker, Paul Dano, Katie Stuart, Bruce Davison,
Nigel Bennett, Terra Vnesa, Sherry Miller, Kim Roberts,
and Andrew Church

Film Synopsis

Too Young to be a Dad is a made-for-television film that provides a unique
perspective on teen pregnancy. It focuses on a 15-year-old boy who finds out
he is going to be a father and how he takes responsibility for his actions.
The film tells the story of Matt Freeman (Paul Dano) and how he prepares
for the birth of his child. Matt transfers schools to be with the mother and
gets a job and starts saving money. The mother's family wants to give the
baby up for adoption; however, Matt struggles with the notion. He eventually receives custody of his daughter.

Terrorism

Terrorism is a very relevant and popular social issue in today's society. Terrorism is simply the act of an individual or group on another for the purpose of creating fear or terror. Films pertaining to terrorism focus on individual acts of terrorism and terrorist groups. Films relevant to terrorism can often pertain to other social issues such as hate groups and racism. However, these social issues are handled separately in this chapter.

Other films dealing with terrorism not detailed in this volume include: *7 Days in September* (2002), *9/11* (2002), *11'09'11—September 11* (2002), *21 Hours at Munich* (1976), *A Wednesday* (2008), *Afghan Stories* (2002), *Black Friday* (2004), *Body of Lies* (2008), *Breaking the Silence: Truth and Lies in the War on Terror* (2003), *Casino Royale* (2006), *Critical Assembly* (2003), *The Delta Force* (1986), *Die Hard* (1988), *Executive Decision* (1996), *Flight 93* (2006), *The Flight that Fought Back* (2005), *Get the Terrorists* (1987), *The Hamburg Cell* (2004), *Harvest of Hate* (1979), *In the Name of the Father* (1994), *Kabul Express* (2006), *The Kingdom* (2007), *Live Free or Die Hard* (2007), *Meltdown* (2004), *Next* (2007), *Nighthawks* (1981), *Oklahoma City: A Survivor's Story* (1998), *On Native Soil* (2006), *One Day in September* (1999), *Path to Paradise: The Untold Story of the World Trade Center Bombing* (1997), *Ransom* (1975), *Rendition* (2007), *The Siege* (1998), *The Sum of all Fears* (2002), *Sword of Gideon* (1989), *Terrorism* (2003), *The Terrorist Next Door* (2008), *Traitor* (2008), *True Lies* (1994), *Under Siege* (1992), *The Voyage of Terror, the Achille Lauro Affair* (1990), *The War Effort* (2003), *Where in the World is Osama Bin Laden?* (2008), *Who Dares Wins* (1982), and *World Trade Center* (2006).

ARLINGTON ROAD

(1999)

Genre: Thriller

MPAA Rating: R

Alternative Title: *Arlington Rd.*

Directed By: Mark Pellington

Produced By: Tom Gorai, Marc Samuelson, and Peter Samuelson

Written By: Ehren Kruger

Color: Color

Length: 117 minutes

Language: English

Production Company: Arlington Road Productions Corporation

Cast: Jeff Bridges, Tim Robbins, Joan Cusack, Hope Davis,
Robert Gossett, Mason Gamble, Darryl Cox, Viviane Vives,
Lee Stringer, and Auden Thornton

Film Synopsis

Arlington Road tells the story of Michael Faraday (Jeff Bridges), a university professor of history who suspects his neighbors are terrorists. Michael gently starts to search for clues that eventually lead him to FBI headquarters. However, a bomb explodes, killing him and 184 others. Michael is blamed for the blast and labeled a terrorist.

FAHRENHEIT 9/11

(2004)

Genre: Documentary

MPAA Rating: R

Alternative Title: *Fahrenheit 911*

Directed By: Michael Moore

Produced By: Jim Czarnecki, Kathleen Glynn, and Michael Moore

Written By: Michael Moore

Color: Color

Length: 122 minutes

Language: English

Production Company: Lions Gate Films

Cast: Michael Moore, Ben Affleck, Stevie Wonder, George W. Bush,
James Baker III, Richard Gephardt, Tom Daschle, Jeffrey Toobin,
Condoleezza Rice, and Al Gore

Film Synopsis

Fahrenheit 9/11 is an award-winning documentary that explores and examines the United States' war on terrorism. The film focuses on the decisions of George W. Bush and the coverage by the American news media on the events surrounding the September 11th attacks and persuasion to invade Iraq in search for Suddam Hussein.

MUNICH

(2005)

Genre: Drama

MPAA Rating: R

Alternative Title: *Untitled 1972 Munich Olympics Project*

Directed By: Steven Spielberg

Produced By: Kathleen Kennedy, Barry Mendel, Steven Spielberg, and Colin Wilson

Written By: Tony Kushner and Eric Roth

Color: Color

Length: 164 minutes

Language: English

Production Company: DreamWorks SKG

Cast: Eric Bana, Daniel Craig, Ciarán Hinds, Mathieu Kassovitz, Hanns Zischler, Ayelet Zurer, Geoffrey Rush, Gila Almagor, and Michael Lonsdale

Film Synopsis

Munich is based on the book, *Vengeance: The True Story of an Israeli Counter-Terrorist Team,* by George Jonas. The film depicts the true story of the 1972 Olympic Games in Munich, where 11 Israeli athletes were taken hostage and murdered by Palestinian terrorists, known as Black September. In retaliation for the murders, the Israeli government recruits Mossad agents to secretly hunt down and execute all involved. *Munich* was nominated for five Academy Awards, including Best Picture and Best Director.

SHOOT ON SIGHT

(2008)

Genre: Crime

MPAA Rating: R

Alternative Title: None

Directed By: Jag Mundhra

Produced By: Aron Govil

Written By: Carl Austin

Color: Color

Length: 129 minutes

Language: English

Production Company: Aron Govil Productions

Cast: Naseeruddin Shah, Greta Scacchi, Alex McSweeney,
    Gulshan Grover, Om Puri, Stephen Greif, Laila Rouass,
    Chris Wilson, and Brian Cox

Film Synopsis

Shoot on Sight is set in London on July 7, 2005, during the London bombings and is based on Operation Kratos, which was the shoot on sight policy that applied to suspected suicide bombers. The film tells the story of a Muslim Scotland Yard police officer named Tariq Ali (Naseeruddin Shah) who is searching for suspected suicide bombers in London.

TERRORSTORM: A HISTORY OF GOVERNMENT-SPONSORED TERRORISM

(2006)

Genre: Documentary

MPAA Rating: Not Rated

Alternative Title: None

Directed By: Alex Jones

Produced By: Alex Jones

Written By: Alex Jones

Color: Color

Length: 113 minutes

Language: English

Production Company: Magnolia Management

Cast: Alex Jones, Ray McGovern, Cindy Sheehan, Steven Jones,
    George W. Bush, Dick Cheney, Michael Hayden,
    and Charlie Sheen

Film Synopsis

TerrorStorm: A History of Government-Sponsored Terrorism is a documentary that examines and explores the notion that governments are guilty of terrorist attacks. The film focuses on how Western governments have committed terrorist attacks on its own people and others throughout history.

UNITED 93

(2006)

Genre: Drama

MPAA Rating: R

Alternative Title: None

Directed By: Paul Greengrass

Produced By: Paul Greengrass, Tim Bevan, Eric Fellner, and Lloyd Levin

Written By: Paul Greengrass

Color: Color

Length: 105 minutes

Language: English

Production Company: Universal Pictures

Cast: J.J. Johnson, Gary Commock, Polly Adams, Trish Gates, Opal Alladin, Starla Benford, David Alan Basche, Richard Bekins, and Denny Dillon

Film Synopsis

United 93 is based on United Airlines Flight 93, which was hijacked by four Islamic terrorists during the September 11, 2001, attacks. The film recounts the events on board the flight and how the heroic passengers overpowered the hijackers and were able to crash the plane in a Pennsylvania field. The film was nominated for two Academy Awards for Best Editing and Best Director.

Women's Rights

The term "women's rights" can be defined as freedoms and entitlements of females of all ages. Most commonly related women's rights issues depicted on film are sexual harassment, sex crimes, suffrage, and equal opportunity (education, employment, and salary). Women's rights issues have been depicted on the big screen throughout its history, but women's rights became an accepted and somewhat popular topic in the last 30–40 years. Films relevant to women's rights can often pertain to other social issues such as abortion, spousal abuse, and teen pregnancy. However, these social issues are handled separately in this chapter.

Other films dealing with the role of government not detailed in this volume include: *Adam's Rib* (1949), *Anchorman: The Legend of Ron Burgundy* (2004), *Antolia* (1995), *Bend It Like Beckham* (2002), *Desk Set* (1957), *Down with Love* (2003), *The Eleanor Roosevelt Story* (1965), *Elizabeth* (1998), *The Face of Rage* (1983), *Flying: Confessions of a Free Woman* (2006), *Girls Rock!* (2007), *I Want to Keep my Baby* (1976), *Kadosh* (1999), *Kate's Secret* (1986), *Kentucky Woman* (1983), *Mona Lisa Smile* (2003), *Moolaade* (2004), *Not for Ourselves Alone: The Story of Elizabeth Cady Stanton & Susan B. Anthony* (1999), *A Place of Rage* (1991), *Policewoman Centerfold* (1983), *Rape & Marriage* (1980), *Roe vs. Wade* (1989), *The Stepford Wives* (2004), *Strike!* (1998), *Thelma & Louise* (1991), *This Child is Mine* (1985), *An Unmarried Woman* (1978), *The Vagina Monologues* (2002), *Vera Drake* (2004), *Victims for Victims* (1984), *When Innocence is Lost* (1997), *Wildcats* (1986), *A Woman Rebels* (1936), *Woman of the Year* (1942), *Women in Chains* (1972), *The Women's Room* (1980), *The World According to Garp* (1982), and *World VDay* (2003).

A BUNNY'S TALE

(1985)

Genre: Drama

MPAA Rating: Not Rated

Alternative Title: None

Directed By: Karen Arthur

Produced By: Stan Margulies

Written By: Deena Goldstone

Color: Color

Length: 104 minutes

Language: English

Production Company: ABC Circle Films

Cast: Kirstie Alley, Joanna Kerns, Lisa Pelikan, Delta Burke, Cotter Smith, and Mary Woronov

Film Synopsis

A Bunny's Tale is based on the true story of Gloria Steinem's personal experience as a Playboy Bunny. Steinem (Kirstie Alley) is writing an article for *Show* magazine and decides to go undercover as a Playboy Bunny in the New York Playboy Club in 1963. The film recounts her undercover assignment and her article, which exposed how women were treated in the Playboy Club.

A LEAGUE OF THEIR OWN

(1992)

Genre: Comedy/Drama

MPAA Rating: PG

Alternative Title: None

Directed By: Penny Marshall

Produced By: Robert Greenhut

Written By: Lowell Ganz and Babaloo Mandel

Color: Color

Length: 128 minutes

Language: English

Production Company: Columbia Pictures Coporation

Cast: Tom Hanks, Geena Davis, Madonna, Lori Petty, Jon Lovitz, Rosie O'Donnell, Bill Pullman, and Garry Marshall

Film Synopsis

A League of Their Own is a fictionalized story about a female baseball team that was part of the real-life All-American Girls Professional Baseball League. The film tells the story of the Rockford Peaches and highlights the relationships among the players and manager. The film also explores the role of female baseball players as athletes and lady-like images. The film was nominated for two Academy Awards for Best Original Song ("This Used To Be My Playground" by Madonna and Shep Pettibone) and Best Actress in a Comedy (Geena Davis).

GRACIE

(2007)

Genre: Drama

MPAA Rating: PG-13

Alternative Title: *Finding Gracie*

Directed By: Davis Guggenheim

Produced By: Davis Guggenheim, Andrew Shue, Elisabeth Shue, and Lemore Syvan

Written By: Lisa Marie Petersen and Karen Janszen

Color: Color

Length: 95 minutes

Language: English

Production Company: Elevation Filmworks

Cast: Carly Schroeder, Jesse Lee Soffer, Elisabeth Shue, Christopher Shand, Karl Girolamo, Donny Gray, Dermot Mulroney, Emma Bell, and Andrew Shue

Film Synopsis

Gracie tells the story of Gracie Brown (Carly Schroeder) and her battle for the right to play soccer. The film is set in 1978 in New Jersey and portrays how Gracie fights for her right to play on the boy's varsity soccer team. Gracie makes her case to the school board, citing the newly passed Title IX law.

IRON JAWED ANGELS

(2004)

Genre: Drama

MPAA Rating: Not Rated

Alternative Title: None

Directed By: Katja von Garnier

Produced By: Lydia Dean Pilcher, Robin Forman, Len Amato, and Paula Weinstein

Written By: Sally Robinson, Eugenia Bostwick-Singer, Raymond Singer, and Jennifer Friedes

Color: Color

Length: 125 minutes

Language: English

Production Company: Home Box Office

Cast: Margo Martindale, Hilary Swank, Anjelica Huston, Lois Smith, Frances O'Connor, Brooke Smith, Molly Parker, and Adilah Barnes

Film Synopsis

Iron Jawed Angels is about the woman's suffrage movement in the early 1900s. The film is based on actual events and tells the story of political activists Alice Paul (Hilary Swank) and Lucy Burns (Frances O'Connor) as they fight for women to have the right to vote. *Iron Jawed Angels* was nominated for three Golden Globes in which it won Best Supporting Actress (Anjelica Huston).

NORTH COUNTRY

(2005)

Genre: Drama

MPAA Rating: R

Alternative Title: *Class Action*

Directed By: Niki Caro

Produced By: Nick Wechsler

Written By: Michael Seitzman

Color: Color

Length: 126 minutes

Language: English

Production Company: Warner Bros. Pictures

Cast: Charlize Theron, Elle Peterson, Thomas Curtis, Frances McDormand, Sean Bean, Woody Harrelson, and Amber Heard

Film Synopsis

North Country is based on the true story surrounding the landmark court case of *Jensen v. Eveleth Taconite Company*. The film tells the story of Josey (Charlize Theron) who works in the mines of northern Minnesota. She and the other female employees are constant victims of sexual harassment and do not receive the same privileges as the male employees. Josey takes legal action and sues her employer. *North Country* is based on the book *Class Action: The Story of Lois Jenson and the Landmark Case That Changed Sexual Harassment Law*, by Clara Bingham and Laura Leedy Gansler. The film was nominated for two Academy Awards for Best Actress (Charlize Theron) and Best Supporting Actress (Frances McDormand).

YENTL

(1983)

Genre: Drama

MPAA Rating: PG

Alternative Title: None

Directed By: Barbra Streisand

Produced By: Rusty Lemorande and Barbra Streisand

Written By: Jack Rosenthal and Barbra Streisand

Color: Color

Length: 132 minutes

Language: English

Production Company: Barwood Films

Cast: Barbra Streisand, Amy Irving, Steven Hill, Mandy Patinkin, Ruth Goring, Nehemiah Persoff, Alan Corduner, and Miriam Margolyes

Film Synopsis

Yentl is set in Poland during a time when women were forbidden to receive an education in Jewish Talmudic law. The film tells the story of a young Jewish girl named Yentl (Barbra Streisand) who decides to live and act like a man so she can learn the Jewish Talmudic law. *Yentl* is based on the play by the same name written by Leah Napolin and Isaac Bashevis Singer. The film was nominated for five Academy Awards, in which it won Best Original Song.

A

Film Ratings

A G-rated motion picture contains nothing in theme, language, nudity, sex, violence, or other matters that, in the view of the Rating Board, would offend parents whose younger children view the motion picture. The G rating is not a "certificate of approval," nor does it signify a "children's" motion picture. Some snippets of language may go beyond polite conversation but they are common everyday expressions. No strong language is present in G-rated motion pictures. Depictions of violence are minimal. No nudity, sex scenes, or drug use are present in the motion picture.

A PG-rated motion picture should be investigated by parents before they let their younger children attend. The PG rating indicates, in the view of the

Teaching Social Issues with Film, pages 163–165
Copyright © 2009 by Information Age Publishing
All rights of reproduction in any form reserved.

Rating Board, that parents may consider some material unsuitable for their children, and parents should make that decision.

The more mature themes in some PG-rated motion pictures may call for parental guidance. There may be some profanity and some depictions of violence or brief nudity, but these elements are not deemed so intense as to require that parents be strongly cautioned beyond the suggestion of parental guidance. There is no drug use content in a PG-rated motion picture.

A PG-13 rating is a sterner warning by the Rating Board to parents to determine whether their children under age 13 should view the motion picture, as some material might not be suitable for them. A PG-13 motion picture may go beyond the PG rating in theme, violence, nudity, sensuality, language, adult activities, or other elements, but does not reach the restricted R category. The theme of the motion picture by itself will not result in a rating greater than PG-13, although depictions of activities related to a mature theme may result in a restricted rating for the motion picture. Any drug use will initially require at least a PG-13 rating. More than brief nudity will require at least a PG-13 rating, but such nudity in a PG-13-rated motion picture generally will not be sexually oriented. There may be depictions of violence in a PG-13 movie, but generally not both realistic and extreme or persistent violence. A motion picture's single use of one of the harsher sexually derived words, though only as an expletive, initially requires at least a PG-13 rating. More than one such expletive requires an R rating, as must even one of those words used in a sexual context. The Rating Board nevertheless may rate such a motion picture PG-13 if, based on a special vote by a two-thirds majority, the raters feel that most American parents would believe that a PG-13 rating is appropriate because of the context or manner in which the words are used or because the use of those words in the motion picture is inconspicuous.

An R-rated motion picture, in the view of the Rating Board, contains some adult material. An R-rated motion picture may include adult themes, adult activity, hard language, intense or persistent violence, sexually oriented nudity, drug abuse, or other elements, so that parents are counseled to take this rating very seriously. Children under age 17 are not allowed to attend R-rated motion pictures unaccompanied by a parent or adult guardian. Parents are strongly urged to find out more about R-rated motion pictures in determining suitability for their children. Generally, it is not appropriate for parents to bring their young children with them to R-rated motion pictures.

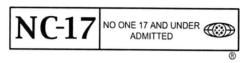

An NC-17-rated motion picture is one that, in the view of the Rating Board, most parents would consider patently too adult for their children age 17 and under. No children will be admitted. NC-17 does not mean "obscene" or "pornographic" in the common or legal meaning of those words, and should not be construed as a negative judgment in any sense. The rating simply signals that the content is appropriate only for an adult audience. An NC-17 rating can be based on violence, sex, aberrational behavior, drug abuse, or any other element that most parents would consider too strong and therefore off-limits for viewing by their children.

Note

Information courtesy of the Motion Picture Association of America (*www.mpaa.org*). Used with permission.

B

Film Analysis Sheet

Title: _____

Year of Production and Rating: _____

Producer: _____

Director: _____

Cast: _____

_____

_____

_____

_____

_____

Major Characters: _____

_____

_____

_____

_____

Synopsis: _____

_____

_____

_____

_____

Issue, event, person, and/or time period portrayed in the film? _____

_____

_____

Is the portrayal accurate? Explain? _____

_____

_____

What are the inaccuracies? _____

_____

_____

Is the portrayal biased? _____

What film techniques are used to intensify the film-viewing experience?

_____

_____

_____

How effective is the film in helping one understand the issue, event, person, and/or time period? Explain? _____

_____

_____

_____

Other relevant information/comments: _____

_____

_____

_____

_____

C

Film Terminology

Audio: The sound portion of the film.

Background Music: Music that accompanies a scene, but not coming from a specific source in the scene.

Boom: A long pole used to hold a camera or microphone.

Camera Angle: The angle in which the camera is pointed (e.g., high-angle shot).

Clip: A short segment of a film.

Close-up: A shot in which an individual's head fills the frame.

Computerized Graphic Imaging (CGI):   Special effects created by a computer and added to the film.

Crane Shot: A camera angle or shot taken from a boom, which allows both horizontal and vertical movement.

Cross-cutting: The method of editing two or more scenes together to portray events that are occurring simultaneously.

Deep Focus: The foreground and background are both in focus simultaneously.

Director: The individual in charge of all aspects of making the film.

Teaching Social Issues with Film, pages 169–171
Copyright © 2009 by Information Age Publishing
169

Dissolve: To fade from one shot while fading in to another shot.

Dolly Shot: A camera shot from a dolly (a camera moving on wheels).

Editing: The process on splicing individual shots together to make a film.

Editor: The individual in charge of splicing the shots together to make a film.

Establishing Shot: A shot that introduces the viewers to the scene.

Extreme Close-up: A shot in which a small detail (e.g., an eyeball) fills the frame.

Extreme Long Shot: A shot in which an individual looks small compared to the landscape in the frame.

Fade: To fade the shot to a black screen or fade a black screen to a shot.

Fast Motion: The movements appear to move at a much faster speed than in real life.

Flashback: A part of the film that deviates from the chronological order and shifts to the past.

Flash Forward: A part of the film that deviates from the chronological order and shifts to the future.

Focus: The sharpness and clarity of an image on the screen.

Frame: The rectangle image projected on the screen.

Freeze Frame: The freezing or stopping of an individual frame.

Genre: The type of film (e.g., drama, biography, or comedy).

High-Angle Shot: A shot from above, which creates a feeling of looking down upon the subject.

Jump Cut: The instant transition from one shot to another.

Lip Sync: The process of aligning the vocals to the actor's mouth movement (aka dubbing).

Long Shot: An entire individual fills the frame.

Low-Angle Shot: A shot from below, which creates a feeling of looking up at the subject.

Medium Long Shot: A shot in which an individual, from the knees up, fills the frame.

Medium Shot: A shot in which an individual, from the waist up, fills the frame.

Pan Shot: The horizontal movement of a shot from side to side.

Point-of-View Shot: A shot from the point of view of one of the subjects in the shot.

Rack-Focus: The camera switches focus between either the background or foreground.

Scene: Multiple shots united by time and space edited together.

Sequence: Multiple scenes untied by time edited together.

Shot: A continuous piece of filming with interruption.

Slow Motion: The movements appear to move at a much slower speed than in real life.

Tilt Shot: An up-or-down shot from a stationary camera.

Voiceover: Narration from a character or narrator that is not seen.

Zoom: The adjustment of the camera lens to bring the images closer or farther away.

References

Allen, W. (1955). Research on film use: Student preparation. *AV Communication Review, 5,* 423–450.

Byford, J., Lennon, S., & Russell, W. (2008). Teaching Controversial Issues in the Social Studies: A Research Study of High School Teachers. *The Clearing House: A Journal of Educational Strategies, Issues, and Ideas, 82*(4), 165–170.

Center for Media Literacy. (2009a). *Media Literacy a Definition…and more.* Retrieved February 15, 2009, from http://www.medialit.org/reading_room/rr2def.php

Center for Media Literacy. (2009b). *10 Benefits of Media Literacy Education.* Retrieved February 15, 2009, from www.medialit.org/reading_room/article667.html

Center for Media Literacy. (2009c). *What is Media Literacy.* Retrieved February 15, 2009, from http://www.medialit.org/reading_room/article675.html

Cotton, R. E. (2006). Teaching controversial environmental issues: neutrality and balance in the reality of the classroom. *Educational Research, 48*(2), 223–241.

Donnelly, M. (2006). Educating students about the Holocaust: A survey of teaching practices. *Social Education, 70*(1), 51–54.

Driscoll, M. P. (2005). *Psychology of learning for instruction.* Needham Heights, MA: Allyn & Bacon.

Engle, S. (2003). Decision-making: The heart of social studies instruction. *The Social Studies 94*(1), 7–10. (Reprinted with permission from *Social Education, 27*(4), 301–304)

Holmes, K., Russell, W., & Movitz, A. (2007). Reading in the social studies: Using subtitled films. *Social Education, 71*(6), 326–330.

Kahne, J., Rodriguez, M., Smith, B.A., & Thiede, K. (2000). Developing citizens for democracy? Assessing opportunities to learn in Chicago's social studies classrooms. *Theory and Research in Social Education, 28*(3), 318–330.

Teaching Social Issues with Film, pages 173–175
Copyright © 2009 by Information Age Publishing
173

Kaiser Family Foundation. (2005). *Generation M: Media in the Lives of 8–18 Years Old.* National Public Study. Retrieved February 15, 2009, from http://www.kff.org.

Leming, J., Ellington, L., & Schug, M. (2006). The state of social studies: A national random survey of elementary and middle school social studies teachers. *Social Education, 70*(5), 322–327.

Levitt, G. A., & Longstreet, W. S. (1993). Controversy and the teaching of authentic civic values. *The Social Studies, 84*(4), 142–147.

Matz, K. A., & Pingatore, L.L. (2005). Reel to reel: Teaching the twentieth century with classic Hollywood films. *Social Education, 69*(4), 189–192.

McGowan, T., McGowan, M., & Lombard, R. (1994). Promoting global perspective. *Social Studies and the Young Learner, 6*(4), 19–22, 29.

Misco, T., & Patterson, N.C. (2007). A study of pre-service teachers' conceptualizations of academic freedom and controversial issues. *Theory and Research in Social Education, 35*(4), 520–550.

National Council for the Social Studies. (2007). *Academic freedom and the social studies teacher.* Retrieved February 15, 2009 from http://www.socialstudies.org/positions/freedom/

Paris, M. (1997). *ERIC clearinghouse for social studies/social science Education.* Bloomington, Indiana. (ERIC Document Reproduction Service No. EDO-SO9714)

Russell, W. (2004). Virtual ideology: Using online political party quizzes, to help students develop a personal political ideology. *Learning and Leading with Technology, 32*(3), 18–21.

Russell, W. (2007a). The Civil War on the silver screen. *Social Studies Review, 47*(1), 21–25.

Russell, W. (2007b). *Using film in the social studies.* Lanham, MD: University Press of America, Inc.

Russell, W. (2008). *Civil War films for teachers and historians.* Lanham, MD: University Press of America.

Soley, M. (1996). If it's controversial, why I teach it? *Social Education 60*(1), 9–14.

Stoddard, J. D., & Marcus, A.S. (2006). The burden of historical representation: Race, freedom, and "educational" Hollywood film. *Film and History, 36*(1), 26–35.

Torney-Purt, J., Lehman, R., Oswald, H., & Schulz, W. (2002). *Citizenship and education in twenty-eight countries.* Amsterdam: International Association for the Evaluation of Education Achievement. Retrieved February 15, 2009, from http//www.wam.umd.edu.iea.

United Nations. (1948). *Convention on the Prevention and Punishment of the Crime of Genocide.* Retrieved February 15, 2009, from http://www.unhchr.ch/html/menu3/b/p_genoci.htm.

United States Copyright Office. (1976). *Title 17 (1) Section 107 of the Copyright Law of the United States; Limitations on exclusive rights: Fair use.* Retrieved February 15, 2009, from http://www.copyright.gov/title17/92chap1.html#107

United States Copyright Office. (1976). *Title 17 (1) Section 110 of the Copyright Law of the United States; Limitations on exclusive rights: Exemption of certain performances and displays.* Retrieved February 15, 2009, from http://www.copyright.gov/title17/92chap1.html#110

United States Government. (1981). Federal guidelines for off-air recording of broadcast programming for educational purposes. *Congressional Record*, pp. E4750–E4752.

Index

Teaching Social Issues with Film, pages 177–175
Copyright © 2009 by Information Age Publishing
    177

LaVergne, TN USA
02 September 2009

156692LV00002B/70/P